# Does the Death Penalty Deter Crime?

Peggy J. Parks

**IN**CONTROVERSY

ReferencePoint Press®

San Diego, CA

**For more information, contact:**
ReferencePoint Press, Inc.
PO Box 27779
San Diego, CA 92198
www.ReferencePointPress.com

Picture credits:
Cover: iStockphoto.com
Maury Aaseng: 23
AP Images: 8, 21, 37, 47, 49, 51, 58, 62, 64, 73, 77
Landov: 29, 43, 70
Photoshot: 13

LIBRARY OF CONGRESS CATALOGING-IN-PUBLICATION DATA

Parks, Peggy J., 1951–
  Does the death penalty deter crime? / by Peggy J. Parks.
    p. cm. — (In controversy)
  Includes bibliographical references and index.
  ISBN-13: 978-1-60152-084-5 (hbk.)
  ISBN-10: 1-60152-084-0 (hbk.)
  1. Capital punishment—United States—Juvenile literature. 2. Punishment in crime deterrence—United States—Juvenile literature. I. Title.
  HV8694.P37 2009
  364.660973—dc22
                                                                    2009017280

# Contents

Foreword                                                            4

Introduction
"Something Is Wrong with Their Reasoning"                           6

Chapter One
What Are the Origins of the Death Penalty
Controversy?                                                        11

Chapter Two
How Do Executions Affect the Crime Rate?                            26

Chapter Three
Does the Legal Process Hamper the Death
Penalty's Deterrence Effect?                                        39

Chapter Four
Does Fear of the Death Penalty Deter Would-Be
Criminals?                                                          54

Chapter Five
Are Alternative Punishments More Effective at
Deterring Crime?                                                    68


Related Organizations                                               80
For Further Research                                                84
Source Notes                                                        87
Index                                                               93
About the Author                                                    96

# Foreword

In 2008, as the U.S. economy and economies worldwide were falling into one of the worst recessions in modern history, most Americans had difficulty comprehending the complexity, magnitude, and scope of what was happening. As is often the case with a complex, controversial issue such as this historic global economic recession, looking at the problem as a whole can be overwhelming and often does not lead to understanding. One way to better comprehend such a large issue or event is to break it into smaller parts. The intricacies of global economic recession may be difficult to understand, but one can gain insight by instead beginning with an individual contributing factor such as the real estate market. When examined through a narrower lens, complex issues become clearer and easier to evaluate.

This is the idea behind ReferencePoint Press's *In Controversy* series. The series examines the complex, controversial issues of the day by breaking them into smaller pieces. Rather than looking at the stem cell research debate as a whole, a title would examine an important aspect of the debate such as *Is Stem Cell Research Necessary?* or *Is Embryonic Stem Cell Research Ethical?* By studying the central issues of the debate individually, researchers gain a more solid and focused understanding of the topic as a whole.

Each book in the series provides a clear, insightful discussion of the issues, integrating facts and a variety of contrasting opinions for a solid, balanced perspective. Personal accounts and direct quotes from academic and professional experts, advocacy groups, politicians, and others enhance the narrative. Sidebars add depth to the discussion by expanding on important ideas and events. For quick reference, a list of key facts concludes every chapter. Source notes, an annotated organizations list, bibliography, and index provide student researchers with additional tools for papers and class discussion.

The *In Controversy* series also challenges students to think critically about issues, to improve their problem-solving skills, and to sharpen their ability to form educated opinions. As President Barack Obama stated in a March 2009 speech, success in the twenty-first century will not be measurable merely by students' ability to "fill in a bubble on a test but whether they possess 21st century skills like problem-solving and critical thinking and entrepreneurship and creativity." Those who possess these skills will have a strong foundation for whatever lies ahead.

No one can know for certain what sort of world awaits today's students. What we can assume, however, is that those who are inquisitive about a wide range of issues; open-minded to divergent views; aware of bias and opinion; and able to reason, reflect, and reconsider will be best prepared for the future. As the international development organization Oxfam notes, "Today's young people will grow up to be the citizens of the future: but what that future holds for them is uncertain. We can be quite confident, however, that they will be faced with decisions about a wide range of issues on which people have differing, contradictory views. If they are to develop as global citizens all young people should have the opportunity to engage with these controversial issues."

*In Controversy* helps today's students better prepare for tomorrow. An understanding of the complex issues that drive our world and the ability to think critically about them are essential components of contributing, competing, and succeeding in the twenty-first century.

# "Something Is Wrong with Their Reasoning"

On December 13, 2005, at 12:35 A.M., Stanley "Tookie" Williams was executed at California's San Quentin State Prison. Williams was the cofounder of the Crips, one of America's most violent street gangs, and his 1979 arrest stemmed from a string of robberies and the murder of 4 people. On death row since 1981, Williams continued to maintain his innocence, stating in a 2005 interview that while he sympathized with the families who had lost loved ones, he was not responsible for the deaths. "In regards to me apologizing," he said, "it would be wrong of me to apologize for something I didn't do. I didn't commit those crimes . . . I cannot apologize for something I didn't do." Williams was then asked to comment on the death penalty and whether he had a message for the people who were fighting to abolish it. "They know that . . . the death penalty isn't a deterrent, and it's not solving any problems," he replied. He added that even with the death penalty in place in many states, the overall prison population throughout the United States was continuing to grow. "If there were a deterrent effect," he said, "then prisons would be empty. We're talking about over 600 on death row in California alone. If a person can deduce from this that the death penalty is working, then something is wrong with their reasoning."[1]

Williams had many supporters outside the prison, including the Reverend Jesse Jackson, actor Jamie Foxx, rapper Snoop Dogg (himself a former Crip), and singer Joan Baez. Those who protested his impending execution cited how Williams had turned his life around while he was incarcerated, including writing a number of books that denounced gang life and warned children about the dangers of crime and violence. His supporters urged that his sentence be commuted to life in prison because if he were allowed to live, he could continue to serve as a positive role model for young people.

There were others, however, who believed that Williams should be executed. Capital punishment supporter and *World Net Daily* founder Joseph Farah was one of them, and he expressed his views just before Williams was put to death. Farah wrote:

> What is it that drives celebrities to the brink of hysteria over the execution death of a quadruple murderer and the founder of a mass-murdering street gang? . . .
>
> Why does one even need to point out the hypocrisy and immorality of holding up this kind of human scum as a role model and hero, while not lifting a finger to memorialize, let alone bring restitution, to the victims of those crimes? . . .
>
> How is it that we have come to live in a world where right is wrong, up is down, black is white and north is south?
>
> It's time for these celebrities to shut up. And it's time for justice to be served—at long last—for Tookie Williams.[2]

After more than 20 years of filing unsuccessful appeals, and the U.S. Supreme Court's refusal to hear his case, Williams was put to death by lethal injection at the age of 51.

## Different Perspectives

The debate over Tookie Williams is just one example of how controversial the capital punishment issue is. Williams was clearly of the mindset that putting criminals to death was not an effective crime deterrent, and many share that viewpoint. Yet numerous others, such as Farah, disagree, arguing that the death penalty does cause would-be criminals to think twice about committing heinous crimes. U.S. district judge Paul G. Cassell refers to two types of deterrence: specific, meaning that once a murderer is apprehended and executed, he or she can never kill again; and

*A supporter displays a poster urging clemency for Crips gang cofounder Stanley "Tookie" Williams. Williams was executed in California in 2005. Before his execution, Williams publicly stated his view that the death penalty does not deter crime.*

general, which refers to the restraining effect the threat of execution has on a much larger pool of potential murderers.

In reference to the viability of general deterrence, Cassell uses the example of John Wojtowicz and 2 accomplices. In 1972, during an attempt to rob Chase Manhattan Bank in New York City, the men held 8 employees hostage for 14 hours. The crime occurred during a period of time when the U.S. Supreme Court had ruled that the death penalty was unconstitutional, so the criminals knew that no matter what they did, they could not legally be put to death. Cassell writes: "In threatening the hostages, Wojtowicz said: 'I'll shoot everyone in the bank. The Supreme Court will let me get away with this. There's no death penalty. It's ridiculous. I can shoot everyone here, then throw my gun down and walk out and they can't put me in the electric chair. You have to have a death penalty, otherwise this can happen everyday.'"[3] Most criminals do not make such impassioned speeches during the commission of a crime, but this example illustrates that at least some have the death penalty on their minds before or during the crime.

Few people believe that it is okay to intentionally kill another person. If putting a murderer to death ensures that he or she will not kill again, however, supporters of the death penalty view this as acceptable. In December 2005 Chicago judge Richard Posner spoke about his belief that the death penalty was a crime deterrent. He said:

> I favor capital punishment because and only because I believe it has "sizeable" deterrent effects. I would join the anti-capital punishment side if this view turns out to be wrong, if it were proven that many innocent persons are wrongly executed, or if it is administered in such a racially biased manner as to wrongly convict many black persons, and to be little used against white murderers. But I do not believe that the available evidence strongly supports any of these arguments against the use of capital punishment.[4]

## An Issue Mired in Controversy

Whether people agree that the death penalty is a "sizeable" crime deterrent or argue that there is no solid proof showing that it deters crime, the one thing most have in common is their passion about the issue. The use of the death penalty has been debated for centuries and remains highly controversial today. While people are deeply divided on many aspects of the death penalty, one that stands out is whether the death penalty deters crime. Many capital punishment advocates are adamant that it does, while others argue that there is no solid evidence to prove it. Although plenty of theories exist, there is no simple way to resolve this issue, largely because of conflicting statistics and a general disagreement over the reliability of evidence. Regardless of how people feel about the death penalty's effectiveness as a crime deterrent, capital punishment is one of the most crucial issues because lives are at stake— the lives of potential victims of violent crime and the lives of those who may face execution for committing the crimes.

## FACTS

• According to the U.S. Department of Justice, 4,995 people were executed in the United States between 1930 and 2008.

• The U.S. Department of Justice reports that 37 people were executed in the United States in 2008. Eighteen executions took place in Texas; 4 in Virginia; 3 each in Georgia and South Carolina; 2 each in Florida, Mississippi, Ohio, and Oklahoma; and 1 in Kentucky.

• Most death penalty laws are state laws, but the federal government has also used capital punishment for offenses such as murder of a government official, a kidnapping that results in death, running a large-scale drug enterprise, and treason.

# What Are the Origins of the Death Penalty Controversy?

For thousands of years the death penalty has been used throughout the world to punish people for various types of criminal acts. In Britain in the 1700s, for instance, more than 200 crimes were punishable by death. These included treason, murder, theft from a shop or house, cutting down a tree, stealing someone's rabbits, refusing to confess to a crime, and marrying a person of the Jewish faith. Capital punishment laws were also enacted in the colonies after Europeans began to settle in America. Because most people believed that convicted criminals deserved to die, these laws were rarely challenged.

Then, during the latter part of the eighteenth century, a group of prominent Americans began to speak out against the death penalty, finding it morally and politically wrong. One of the most outspoken was a physician named Benjamin Rush, who was one of the country's founders and a signer of the Declaration of Independence. Rush wrote several essays during the 1780s and 1790s in which he denounced capital punishment and called for it to be outlawed. In one of the essays, entitled "Abolish the Absurd and Unchristian Practice," Rush wrote: "I have said nothing upon the manner of inflicting death as a punishment for crimes, because I consider it as an improper

11

punishment for *any* crime. Even murder itself is propagated by the punishment of death for murder."[5] In using the word *propagated*, Rush was referring to cities such as Rome where the death penalty was in place and executions were public. These executions, he stated, led to significantly more murders than in the neighboring region of Tuscany, where criminals were not executed and violent crime, especially murder, was less frequent.

## Early Influences

Although Rush was one of the most famous death penalty opponents of his time, controversy over the issue had been brewing in Europe years before he began speaking and writing about his beliefs. One of the most prominent European objectors was French philosopher and essayist François-Marie Arouet (better known by his pen name of Voltaire), who in 1762 wrote a stinging commentary in which he expressed his contempt for western Europe's prolific use of capital punishment: "Christian tribunals have condemned to death more than 100,000 so-called witches. If you add to these . . . massacres the infinitely higher number of heretics [executed by fire], this part of the world will be seen as nothing other than a vast scaffold crowded with executioners and their victims, surrounded by judges and spectators."[6] Voltaire's writings proved to be a powerful motivator for those who wanted the death penalty abolished, and more people began to speak out against a practice that they viewed as cruel and barbaric, as well as totally ineffective as a crime deterrent.

Even more influential than Voltaire was an Italian philosopher and criminologist named Cesare Beccaria, who wrote an essay in 1767 titled "Of Crimes and Punishments." He used strong language to convey his conviction that there was no justification for the intentional killing of a human being even if the person has committed crimes. Beccaria said that the death penalty was "pernicious to society, from the example of barbarity it affords," and then asked: "What *right* . . . have men to cut the throats of their fellow creatures? Certainly not that on which the sovereignty and laws are founded." Calling the death penalty "a war of a whole nation against a citizen whose destruction they consider as necessary or useful to the general good,"[7] he claimed that it was neither necessary nor useful because it was not a deterrent to crime.

Beccaria referred to years of experience that had proved "the punishment of death has never prevented determined men from injuring society." His contention was that a much more effective

Eighteenth-century Italian philosopher Cesare Beccaria argued that execution is less of a deterrent than life imprisonment. His thoughts on the subject appeared in the essay "Of Crimes and Punishments." A title page from the work is shown.

punishment would be lifetime imprisonment, which he referred to as "perpetual slavery." He wrote:

> The death of a criminal is a terrible but momentary spectacle, and therefore a less efficacious method of deterring others than the continued example of a man deprived of his liberty, condemned, as a beast of burden, to repair, by his labour, the injury he has done to society, *If I commit such a crime*, says the spectator to himself, *I shall be reduced to that miserable condition for the rest of my life.* A much more powerful preventive than the fear of death which men always behold in distant obscurity.[8]

## Reforms

Beccaria made a humble reference to himself in the essay, professing his belief that "the voice of one philosopher is too weak to be heard amidst the clamours of a multitude, blindly influenced by custom."[9] He was not, however, viewed as merely one philosopher. In fact, he had no way of knowing how influential his writing would become over the following decades in shaping public opinion. Rush was influenced by Beccaria's writings, as was Thomas Jefferson, who attempted to reform Virginia's death penalty in the late 1700s. Jefferson introduced a bill that would change the law to impose capital punishment only on those who had committed murder or treason, but the bill was defeated by one vote. Thus, Virginia continued to execute people for offenses such as burglary, slave revolt, horse stealing, arson, rape, and piracy, as well as murder and attempted murder.

In the early part of the nineteenth century, many states began to revise their capital punishment laws. Some reduced the number of crimes that were punishable by death. Others passed laws that outlawed public hangings, which were common during that time. Pennsylvania and Rhode Island were the first to abolish public executions, followed by New York, Massachusetts, and New Jersey. By 1849, 10 other states had done the same, and Michigan had become the first state

"I have said nothing upon the manner of inflicting death as a punishment for crimes, because I consider it as an improper punishment for any crime."[5]

— Founding father and signer of the Declaration of Independence, Benjamin Rush.

## What Europeans Think About the Death Penalty's Deterrence Effect

In April 2007 the Associated Press polled residents of several European countries that do not have capital punishment laws in place. Respondents were asked the question, "If the death penalty were implemented in [your country], do you think the number of murders would go up, go down, or stay about the same?" Only 2 percent of those from France thought murders would go up; 37 percent thought they would go down, 59 percent thought they would stay about the same, and 2 percent were not sure. Respondents from Germany had even less favorable views about the death penalty. Three percent said murders would increase, 22 percent said they would decrease, 73 percent said the murder rate would stay about the same, and 2 percent said they were unsure. Opinions of those from Spain and Italy were virtually identical, with 51 percent saying they felt the death penalty would have little or no effect on the murder rate.

to abolish the death penalty completely except for cases of treason.

A move that capital punishment opponents saw as a major victory occurred in 1838 when Tennessee and Alabama passed discretionary death penalty statutes. These laws represented a radical change because prior to their passage, the federal government mandated execution for anyone who was convicted of a crime that was punishable by death (known as a capital crime), regardless of the circumstances. Now the two states had the freedom to make their own decisions about which criminals would and would not be put to death. By 1895 a total of 18 states had such discretionary statutes in place.

The early part of the 1900s was known as the Progressive Era in American politics, during which more states began to revise their laws or repeal them altogether. Historian and author

Gary P. Gershman describes this period of time and the mindset of those who wanted the death penalty repealed:

> The number of federal offenses that were considered capital crimes diminished, so that only four remained. The Progressives felt they had an ability to change the world, because they believed that evils in society were the result of nurture not nature. Therefore, they reasoned, if drinking were eliminated, society would improve. If the environment were changed, people would not find it necessary to resort to crime, and therefore would not have to be expunged from society.[10]

By 1917, largely because of the influence of the Progressive movement, a total of nine states had abolished the death penalty.

## Twentieth-Century Changes

The United States' trend away from capital punishment began to shift during the 1920s. Prohibition, which made it illegal to manufacture or distribute alcohol, was put into effect in 1919 with Congress's ratification of the Eighteenth Amendment to the Constitution. Although the intent of the law was to reduce people's dependence on alcohol and cut down on crime, the opposite occurred. Violent gangs of mobsters began to build their fortunes on distributing liquor, and crime soared—between 1915 and 1933 the homicide rate in America nearly doubled. *Wall Street Journal* writer Cynthia Crossen refers to these years as a time when "criminals became better armed, more mobile and more brazen." She describes the state of the country:

> During the 1920s and early 1930s, Americans were shocked by the spectacular crimes of such "public enemies" as Pretty Boy Floyd, Baby Face Nelson and Ma Barker's gang. In 1932 Charles Lindbergh Jr., son of one of the country's most loved heroes, was snatched from his crib and murdered. The following year, four police officers and their prisoner were gunned down in public in what became known as the Kansas City Massacre.[11]

Because crime was running rampant in the United States, support for capital punishment began to soar, and 6 of the states that had abolished the death penalty reinstated it. During the 1930s more criminals were put to death than any other decade in American history—an average of 167 executions per year over the 10-year period, with an all-time high of 199 executions in 1935.

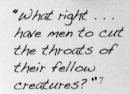

"What right . . . have men to cut the throats of their fellow creatures?"[7]

— Italian philosopher and criminologist Cesare Beccaria.

Yet even as the execution rate in the United States was spiking and Americans expressed widespread public support for capital punishment, other countries were starting to change their death penalty laws. In 1949 Great Britain established the Royal Commission on Capital Punishment, whose assignment was to evaluate whether the death penalty should be modified or abolished. After completing exhaustive investigations, the group determined that there was no proof that executing convicted criminals deterred crime. After publication, the results of the investigations received widespread publicity, as historian Philip English Mackey writes: "Books and articles about their findings were plentiful. One such book was Arthur Koestler's *Reflections on Hanging*, which saw wide circulation in the United States. In the preface to the American edition, New York University law professor Edmond Cahn exhorted his countrymen to abolish executions."[12]

Public opinion in the United States was also influenced by the crime rate, which had steadily decreased after Prohibition was repealed—by 1943 the number of homicides was even lower than it had been in 1915. This caused many to rethink whether capital punishment was necessary, and it also led to a dramatic reduction in executions, as the Death Penalty Information Center explains: "Whereas there were 1,289 executions in the 1940s, there were 715 in the 1950s, and the number fell even further, to only 191, from 1960 to 1976. In 1966 support for capital punishment reached an all-time low."[13] This waning public support became apparent during a 1966 Gallup poll, which showed that only 42 percent of Americans supported the death penalty, compared with 61 percent who were in favor of it in 1936.

# Supreme Court Rulings

As more people in the United States voiced their objections to capital punishment, some states responded by repealing or revising their laws. During the 1960s Michigan abolished the death penalty for treason, and Iowa, Oregon, New York, West Virginia, Vermont, and New Mexico all repealed their death penalty legislation. Capital punishment opponents began focusing their efforts on the courts, which they believed would be a more effective conduit for getting the death penalty abolished rather than trying to accomplish it state by state.

Prior to the 1960s the Supreme Court had on several occasions ruled that the death penalty was not in violation of the Constitution. In November 1946, for instance, the Court heard the case *Francis v. Resweber*, which challenged that the death penalty violated the Eighth Amendment's prohibition of cruel and unusual punishment. The case involved a defendant who had been placed in the electric chair and was severely shocked but survived electrocution because of faulty equipment. He was returned to his cell and again scheduled for execution 6 days later. The lawsuit alleged that he had been subjected to cruel and unusual punishment and, therefore, his life should be spared. The Court disagreed. In a 5 to 4 ruling, the justices declared that it would be constitutional to continue with the execution. They wrote:

> Even the fact that petitioner has already been subjected to a current of electricity does not make his subsequent execution any more cruel in the constitutional sense than any other execution. The cruelty against which the Constitution protects a convicted man is cruelty inherent in the method of punishment, not the necessary suffering involved in any method employed to extinguish life humanely. . . . The situation of the unfortunate victim of this accident is just as though he had suffered the identical amount of mental anguish and physical pain in any other occurrence, such as, for example, a fire in the cell block.

"If the environment were changed, people would not find it necessary to resort to crime, and therefore would not have to be expunged from society."[10]

— Historian and author Gary P. Gershman.

We cannot agree that the hardship imposed upon the petitioner rises to that level of hardship denounced as denial of due process because of cruelty.[14]

In the years following the *Francis v. Resweber* case, other lawsuits were filed that challenged the legality of the death penalty. The 1960s was a time when the anti-death-penalty movement began to gain strength, as U.S. circuit court of appeals judge Alexander Kozinski explains:

Up to that point, reduction in capital statutes and their complete abolition had been undertaken exclusively by

## "Evolving Standards of Decency"

In 1958 the Supreme Court ruled on a case that involved stripping someone of U.S. citizenship. An army private had been court-martialed and given a dishonorable discharge for desertion during World War II. He was later denied the ability to obtain a passport because he was a convicted wartime deserter, which, in effect, meant that he was no longer officially an American citizen. The Court ruled in his favor because the justices said the punishment did not fit the crime and was therefore unconstitutional. In the ruling Chief Justice Earl Warren wrote that the Eighth Amendment contained "evolving standards of decency that mark the progress of a maturing society." Warren was saying that as society had continued to evolve, it had become clear that the Constitution mandated dignified treatment of all citizens, including criminals, and it was up to the Court to ensure that punishments were not unduly cruel or excessive in relation to the crime. Though the case had no connection to the death penalty, capital punishment opponents seized on Warren's "standards of decency" language as a rationale for why the country should no longer tolerate the death penalty.

Quoted in Cornell University Law School, "Supreme Court Collection: *Trop v. Dulles* (No. 70)." www.law.cornell.edu.

state legislatures and Congress. Beginning in 1967, lawyers attacked the death penalty on constitutional grounds, arguing that it violated "due process of law," "equal protection of the law," and especially the prohibition against "cruel and unusual punishment." These challenges resulted in a de facto moratorium on executions, as the Supreme Court wrestled with their arguments.[15]

In another case in 1968, *Witherspoon v. Illinois*, the Court addressed an Illinois statute that allowed for the dismissal of any jury members who opposed capital punishment or had even slight doubts about it. At the trial, prosecutors had used the statute to eliminate half of the prospective jurors without determining whether their views on the death penalty would prevent them from being unbiased. The Court denounced this, declaring that a juror could only be disqualified if the prosecution could show that his or her attitude toward capital punishment would preclude the ability to make an impartial decision. The justices wrote:

> A man who opposes the death penalty, no less than one who favors it, can make the discretionary choice of punishment entrusted to him by the State, and can thus obey the oath he takes as a juror; but in a nation where so many have come to oppose capital punishment, a jury from which all such people have been excluded cannot perform the task demanded of it—that of expressing the conscience of the community on the ultimate question of life or death.[16]

## A Victory for the Opposition

After years of challenging the constitutionality of the death penalty, opponents scored a major victory on June 29, 1972. In a case known as *Furman v. Georgia*, the Supreme Court declared that in order for a punishment to be constitutional, it needed to meet certain criteria: It could not be more severe than the crime warranted, it could not be given based on arbitrary reasons, and it could not offend society's sense of justice. The Court stated

*In the 1940s, a death row inmate challenged the legality of the electric chair, arguing that this form of execution represented cruel and unusual punishment. The U.S. Supreme Court disagreed with that assertion. Virginia's electric chair is shown here in 2006.*

that the way Georgia's death penalty laws were written, juries had total discretion over sentencing guidelines. This, according to the justices, could easily lead to discrimination, which is banned under the Fourteenth Amendment. In a vote of five to four, the Court ruled that the death penalty was in direct violation of both the Eighth and Fourteenth Amendments. In its written statement, the Court said: "It would seem to be incontestable that the death penalty inflicted on one defendant is 'unusual' if it discriminates against him by reason of his race, religion, wealth, social position, or class, or if it is imposed under a procedure that gives room for the play of such prejudices." Later in the document the Court explained why Georgia's death penalty laws were unconstitutional: "They are pregnant with discrimination and discrimination is an ingredient not compatible with the idea of equal protection of the laws that is implicit in the ban on 'cruel and unusual' punishments."[17] Following the landmark decision, the Court nullified all state death penalty statutes, and the sentences of all death row inmates throughout the United States were commuted to life in prison.

## A Turning Point

The de facto moratorium that had begun in the mid-1960s was now an official moratorium on the death penalty that would last for several more years. By invalidating the capital punishment laws of the states, the Supreme Court had brought all criminal executions to a halt, and this presented opportunities for the death penalty's deterrence effect to be studied. Unlike any other time in history, researchers could now examine homicide statistics and compare them with periods of time when capital punishment laws were in place. According to the U.S. Department of Justice's Bureau of Justice Statistics, during the years when the death penalty was not in effect, homicides increased. In 1967, for instance, the number of murders in the United States was 6.8 per 100,000 people, and by 1974 it had risen to 9.8 per 100,000.

The Supreme Court's *Furman v. Georgia* ruling had another effect as well. Because the majority of justices had ruled that certain death penalty statutes were unconstitutional, this opened the door for states to revise their laws in order to be in full compliance with the Constitution. Most of them began to do this, as the Death

"*The cruelty against which the Constitution protects a convicted man is cruelty inherent in the method of punishment, not the necessary suffering involved in any method employed to extinguish life humanely.*"[14]

— The Supreme Court, in announcing its ruling on the 1946 case *Francis v. Resweber.*

Penalty Information Center explains: "Advocates of capital punishment began proposing new statutes that they believed would end arbitrariness in capital sentencing. The states were led by Florida, which rewrote its death penalty statute only five months after *Furman*. Shortly after, 34 other states proceeded to enact new death penalty statutes."[18]

Over the following years other capital punishment lawsuits were heard by the Supreme Court. In one of them, *Gregg v. Georgia*, the

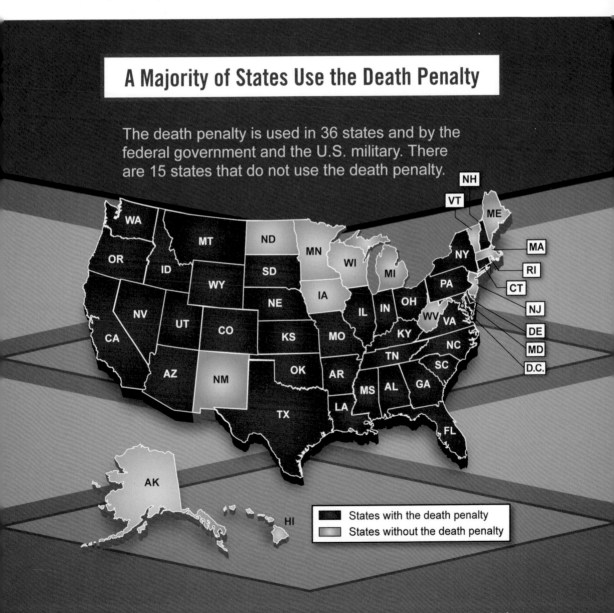

# A Majority of States Use the Death Penalty

The death penalty is used in 36 states and by the federal government and the U.S. military. There are 15 states that do not use the death penalty.

States with the death penalty
States without the death penalty

justices ruled that Georgia's revised death penalty no longer violated the Constitution, and similar pronouncements were later made about laws in Florida, Texas, Utah, and Oklahoma. By 1976, 36 states had revised their death penalty statutes in order to comply with the Supreme Court's ruling, and in doing so made capital punishment once again legal.

After years of waning support for the death penalty, public approval soared during the 1980s and 1990s. A 1994 Gallup poll revealed that 80 percent of respondents were in favor of capital punishment for people convicted of murder—an all-time high. Yet public opinion has widely fluctuated since that time. A poll conducted in 2001 showed that the approval rate for the death penalty had dropped to 67 percent, whereas by October 2007 it had risen slightly to 69 percent. Opinions on the death penalty's deterrent effect are also mixed. In a February 2008 Harris poll, 42 percent of respondents said they believed that executing people who commit murder deters others from committing murder, while 52 percent said such executions did not have much deterrence effect.

## The Debate Rages On

The death penalty is as controversial today as it has been throughout history. According to Amnesty International, 59 countries still allow capital punishment, but many others have repealed death penalty laws over the years. In Europe, for instance, the only country that still has such laws in effect is the tiny nation of Belarus, a former Soviet republic. As of April 2009, 36 U.S. states, as well as the federal government and the military, had death penalty legislation in place, although some states have been contemplating whether the laws should be revised or abolished. As much, and as often, as public opinion has varied on the death penalty issue over the years, the debate involves many difficult questions. Central among these questions is whether the death penalty deters would-be criminals from committing murder. How people feel about this and other related issues often depends more on their own personal viewpoints about the death penalty than on what statistics show.

- In 1888 New York became the first state to build and use an electric chair for executions.

- The first criminal to be executed in the United States after the death penalty was ruled constitutional by the Supreme Court during the 1970s was Gary Gilmore, a murderer who was killed by firing squad in Utah in January 1977.

- In 1977 the Supreme Court ruled that the use of the death penalty in rape cases was unconstitutional, which resulted in the removal of 20 inmates from death row.

- In a May 2006 Gallup poll, respondents were asked whether they believe the death penalty acts as a deterrent to murder and lowers the homicide rate; 34 percent said it does deter, 64 percent said that it does not, and 2 percent were unsure.

- The homicide rate in the United States is five to seven times higher than in European countries that do not have the death penalty.

# CHAPTER TWO

# How Do Executions Affect the Crime Rate?

As someone who worked in the corrections field for 30 years and served for several years as warden of San Quentin Prison in California, Jeanne Woodford is well acquainted with criminals and crime. During her tenure as chief executive of the prison, she presided over four executions. "After each one," she writes, "someone on the staff would ask, 'Is the world safer because of what we did tonight?' We knew the answer: No."[19] Woodford makes it clear that she is not soft on crime—far from it. But after her many years of witnessing criminal behavior and executions, she is convinced that the death penalty is not a deterrent to crime and therefore does not result in a lower crime rate.

In fact, Woodford says, it is exponentially more expensive to keep prisoners on death row and execute them than to incarcerate them for life, as the former depletes money that could be put to better use preventing and fighting crime. She explains:

> If we condemn the worst offenders . . . to permanent imprisonment, resources now spent on the death penalty could be used to investigate unsolved homicides, modernize crime labs and expand effective violence prevention

programs, especially in at-risk communities. The money also could be used to intervene in the lives of children at risk and to invest in their education—to stop future victimization.[20]

## Early Studies

Woodford is far from alone in her assertion that the death penalty does not result in a reduced crime rate—many share her viewpoint. But there are numerous others who disagree, claiming that there is a direct correlation between executions and decreased criminal activities. One of the first to propose this theory was Isaac Ehrlich in his 1975 article, "The Deterrent Effect of Capital Punishment: A Question of Life and Death." Using a statistical technique known as econometrics (which combines economics with mathematics) to analyze murder and execution rates over more than three decades, Ehrlich determined that capital punishment was a significant deterrent to homicides. He wrote:

"*The accumulated scientific evidence from these later studies also weighed heavily against the claim that executions deter murders.*"[22]

— Columbia University law professor Jeffrey Fagan.

> Contrary to previous observations, this investigation, although by no means definitive, does indicate the existence of a pure deterrent effect of capital punishment. In fact, the empirical analysis suggests that on the average the tradeoff between the execution of an offender and the lives of potential victims it might have saved was of the order of magnitude of 1 for 8 for the period 1933–67 in the United States.[21]

Because Ehrlich's article appeared in *American Economic Review*, it was written in highly technical language, and its target audience was economists—yet the article's influence spread far beyond the economics community. Columbia University law professor Jeffrey Fagan writes: "Ehrlich's work was cited in *Gregg v. Georgia*, the central U.S. Supreme Court decision restoring capital punishment. No matter how carefully Ehrlich qualified his conclusions, his article had the popular and political appeal of a headline, a sound bite and a bumper sticker all rolled into one." Fagan goes on to say that Ehrlich's article drew widespread criticism, including being denounced by contributors to the *Yale Law Journal*, as well as by the National Academy of Sciences. This, says Fagan, launched

> an era of contentious arguments in the press and in professional journals. . . . Over the next two decades, economists and other social scientists attempted (mostly without success) to replicate Ehrlich' s results using different data, alternative statistical methods, and other twists that tried to address glaring errors in Ehrlich's techniques and data. The accumulated scientific evidence from these later studies also weighed heavily against the claim that executions deter murders.[22]

One of Ehrlich's students, economist Stephen Layson, was not at all convinced that his mentor's research was flawed, and he decided to expand on Ehrlich's studies. After completing his own analysis, in which he compared the number of executions in the United States with the total number of homicides committed between 1933 and 1977, Layson wrote an article that was published in the July 1985 issue of *Southern Economic Journal*. He first critically examined and refuted the accusations that Ehrlich's findings were incorrect, and then he corroborated the theory that capital punishment deterred crime. In fact, Layson went further than Ehrlich, stating that on average, each execution in the United States prevented approximately 18 murders.

Following the publication of these findings, judges Stephen Markman and Paul Cassell wrote an article that appeared in a 1988 issue of Stanford University's law review. Touting the credibility of Layson's analysis, Markman and Cassell concluded that the death penalty had deterred "roughly 125,000 murders in this country in [the twentieth] century." They went on to say that the research "demonstrates rather starkly that under any realistic risk assessment the presence of capital punishment saves more innocent lives than it jeopardizes."[23]

## "Not Closely Associated"

Those who argue against the perspective shared by Layson, Markman, and Cassell often claim that the statistics cited by researchers are inadequate to prove that the death penalty actually deters crime. According to professors Cass R. Sunstein and Justin Wolfers, when all the evidence is considered, one cannot necessarily conclude that the death penalty is or is not a deterrent to murder, as both claims are extremely difficult to prove. Sunstein and Wolfers write:

> The number of homicides is so large, and varies so much year to year, that it is impossible to disentangle the effects of execution policy from other changes affecting murder

*A Boston police officer searches a passenger during a traffic stop. Experts say that crime rates increase where drug dealers and gangs proliferate and decrease where police have a strong presence. These factors complicate efforts to determine the death penalty's deterrent effect.*

rates. Moreover, execution policy doesn't change often or much. Just as a laboratory scientist with too few experimental subjects cannot draw strong conclusions, the best we can say is that homicide rates are not closely associated with capital punishment. On the basis of existing evidence, it is especially hard to justify claims about causality.[24]

The reference by Sunstein and Wolfers to "other changes" that affect the number of homicides is important because many factors can influence a rise or fall in the murder rate. For instance, when unemployment is high and people struggle economically, murders and other violent crime tend to increase. An increase in crime is also common when drug dealers and gangs become more prevalent in cities and neighborhoods. Conversely, when law enforcement presence is stronger and neighborhood watch groups are active, the result is often a drop in violent crime. For instance, between 2005 and 2006 the homicide rate decreased 20 percent in New York City and 19 percent in Los Angeles, and among cities with populations over 1 million, murder rates dropped 9.8 percent. Criminologists attribute this to several factors, as *U.S. News & World Report* journalist Emma Schwartz explains: "Major cities have more sophisticated policing methods and more resources to respond to any fluctuations in crime rates."[25]

In an April 2006 paper written by Justin Wolfers and John J. Donohue, the authors refer to Ehrlich's research and his subsequent conclusion that the death penalty deters crime. They claim that he left out important data that, had it been included, would have resulted in very different findings. For instance, in Ehrlich's analysis of the connection between executions and murder rates, he failed to note that between the late 1930s and 1960, executions dropped by 80 percent—and over that same period of time there was a sharp decline in the murder rate. Another consideration Wolfers and Donohue point out is that a decline in homicides during the mid-1960s occurred in all states, including those where death penalty statutes were not in effect at the time.

"*Just as a laboratory scientist with too few experimental subjects cannot draw strong conclusions, the best we can say is that homicide rates are not closely associated with capital punishment.*"[24]

— Cass R. Sunstein, law professor at Harvard Law School and Justin Wolfers, assistant professor of business and public policy at the University of Pennsylvania's Wharton School.

## The Challenge of Interpreting Statistics

Researchers have studied the connection between the death penalty and crime rates for decades, with some concluding there is a clear deterrent effect and others concluding the opposite. Richard Berk, a researcher in the Department of Statistics at the University of California–Los Angeles, says it may never be possible to make an accurate determination about this—one way or the other. Berk examined numerous studies involving the death penalty and crime rates and presented his findings in a March 2005 paper. According to Berk:

> The analyses reported here are hardly exhaustive and are perhaps affected by misunderstandings about the data provided, or by errors in the data themselves. Nevertheless, the results raise serious questions about whether anything useful about the deterrent value of the death penalty can ever be learned from an observational study with the data that are likely to be available.

Richard Berk, *New Claims About Executions and General Deterrence: Déjà Vu All Over Again?* March 11, 2005. http://preprints.stat.ucla.edu.

In further examining the effects of the death penalty on the murder rate, Wolfers and Donohue draw a comparison between the United States and Canada. "The most striking finding," they write, "is that the homicide rate in Canada has moved in virtual lockstep with the rate in the United States, while approaches to the death penalty have diverged sharply."[26] Until the 1950s both countries had death penalty legislation in place, and the homicide trends were similar. Then in 1961 Canada restricted the use of the death penalty to those who committed premeditated murder or killed a police officer, and six years later revised it again to apply only to those who murdered an officer in the line of duty.

As a result of these capital punishment restrictions, no one has been executed in Canada since 1962—yet homicides have not increased and are still in line with those of the United States. Donohue and Wolfers write: "The *Furman* case in 1972 led to a death penalty moratorium in the United States. While many death penalty advocates attribute the subsequent sharp rise in homicides to this moratorium, a similar rise is equally evident in Canada, which was obviously unaffected by this U.S. Supreme Court decision."[27]

They add that in 1976 the capital punishment policies of the two countries diverged even more sharply. The Supreme Court's *Gregg v. Georgia* ruling led to the reinstatement of the death penalty in the United States, while Canadian officials abolished the death penalty altogether. Over the two decades that followed Canada's repeal of its capital punishment laws, the country's homicide rates fell. "The Canadian move towards abolition is also interesting," write Donohue and Wolfers, "because it represented a major policy shock: prior to abolition, the proportion of murderers executed in Canada was considerably higher than that in the United States."[28]

## Some Argue Studies Show Deterrence

Donohue and Wolfers reject the notion that a rise or fall in crime can be directly connected with the death penalty, but they do not deny that such a connection is possible. Their argument, rather, is that because the evidence presented has thus far been inconclusive or even badly flawed at times, a definitive causal relationship cannot yet be shown. There are others, however, who claim that their own studies have proved the opposite to be true. Louisiana State University economics professor Naci Mocan coauthored a study in 2003 and then reexamined the data in 2006. He concluded that each execution in the United States resulted in five fewer homicides, and when a death sentence was commuted, this resulted in five additional homicides. "Science does really draw a conclusion," he says. "It did. There is no question about it. The conclusion is there is a deterrent effect."[29]

Mocan's study involved analyzing executions and murders that took place by year, as well as by state or county, in an effort to determine capital punishment's effect on the crimes. He also factored in other data such as unemployment statistics, per capita income, and arrest and conviction probabilities, among other relevant factors. "The results are robust, they don't really go away," he says. "I oppose the death penalty. But my results show that the death penalty deters—what am I going to do, hide them?"[30]

Another study was published in November 2007 by the late Roy D. Adler and Michael Summers, who were both professors at Pepperdine University in Malibu, California. Adler and Summers analyzed criminal activity and executions over a 26-year period between 1979 to 2004. After comparing the number of executions in the United States with the number of homicides that had been committed during the same time, they found a direct correlation between capital punishment and the future murder rate. According to their research, when executions increased, homicides decreased the following year. Conversely, when executions leveled off, the murder rate spiked the following year.

After their analysis was complete, Adler and Summers determined that each execution was associated with 74 fewer murders. Adler stated that neither of them had any particular agenda in doing the research, as he explained: "The morality of the issue is something for someone else to argue. We're just simply presenting the data and lifting the veil that says, 'There's no deterrent effect . . .' Well, there is, and it's about 74 to 1. And other people can argue moral grounds on either side." Adler added that the crucial question is not whether the murderer's life should be spared, but rather, whether to spare the lives of innocent people who could be victims the following year. "Our intent was to open this up to a dialogue," he said. "The ratio is not 'save a life or not'; it's 'save this life or save dozens of others next year.' And that's a much more difficult moral dilemma that deserves wide discussion, I think."[31]

"I oppose the death penalty. But my results show that the death penalty deters [crime]—what am I going to do, hide them?"[30]

— Louisiana State University economics professor Naci Mocan.

## Analyzing State Trends

Studies such as those by Adler and Summers appear to be conclusive, and the authors have no doubt that they have proved a correlation between executions and the crime rate. Yet these findings do

## "Many Factors Influence Crime Rates"

Since the 1970s when Isaac Ehrlich concluded that the death penalty was a deterrent to homicide, other researchers have arrived at similar findings. This is controversial for many reasons, one of which is the likelihood that numerous other factors influence rising or falling violent crime rates, including murder. According to Barry Krisberg, who is president of the National Council on Crime and Delinquency research institute, people often assume that crime will be reduced if prisoners are taken off the streets, but "the evidence for this is much more ambiguous," he writes. "Many factors influence crime rates, such as demographics, immigration patterns, unemployment rates, epidemics of illegal drugs and guns, housing density and policing strategies, among other variables." Krisberg adds that another influencer is national crime trends. "During the period when California's crime rate was going down, there was a general national trend toward lower crime rates in almost every state.

Barry Krisberg, "Crime vs. Punishment," *Los Angeles Times*, August 7, 2007. www.latimes.com.

not convince death penalty opponents, who point to differences among states that do and do not have capital punishment laws in effect. According to statistics from the Death Penalty Information Center and the U.S. Department of Justice, between 1990 and 2007, states without the death penalty had lower homicide rates every year than those with the death penalty. In 1996, for instance, non-death-penalty states had 44 percent fewer murders, and in 2006 the difference reached an all-time high of 46 percent. This, says the Death Penalty Information Center, is tangible proof that the death penalty does not deter crime—in fact, based on these figures, executions have an inverse effect, actually resulting in higher murder rates.

Yet Sunstein and Wolfers challenge such a definitive conclusion. "What does the evidence actually say?" they ask. "One approach notes that in states with the death penalty, the average murder rate is about 40 percent higher than in states without the death penalty. Yet such comparisons are surely confounded by other influences, as those states that impose the death penalty also have a historic culture of violence, including lynching."[32]

Cassell agrees that many factors must be taken into consideration when comparing murder rates among states. He claims that death penalty opponents do not thoroughly examine the statistics, and "when they trouble to do so, they typically do little more than assert that the states without the death penalty have lower homicide rates than states with the penalty." Cassell refers to this type of analysis as "fundamentally flawed"[33] because, as Sunstein and Wolfers point out, it fails to take into account regional differences such as criminal justice expenditures, economic prosperity, educational levels, and other factors that are known potentially to influence homicide rates.

To better understand Cassell's reasoning, it is useful to analyze the homicide rates of states that are often used by death penalty opponents as examples of why capital punishment is not a crime deterrent. For instance, two states that do not have capital punishment laws in place are Alaska and Hawaii, and their murder rates are extremely low. This is true of some other non-death-penalty states as well. But whether the lack of executions can in any way be correlated with the number of homicides is questionable because these states have historically been known for their low crime rates. University of Maryland scientist John Lott explains: "This simple comparison really doesn't prove anything. The . . . states without the death penalty have long enjoyed relatively low murder rates due to factors unrelated to capital punishment."[34] One must also consider New Hampshire, where death penalty legislation is in place and which, according to the U.S. Department of Justice, has the lowest homicide rate of any state in the country.

When capital punishment opponents opine that murder rates are highest in states that have death penalty legislation, they often point

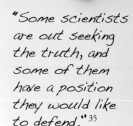

"Some scientists are out seeking the truth, and some of them have a position they would like to defend."[35]

— Emory University economist Paul Rubin.

to southern states where the most executions take place. For instance, Texas, Virginia, Oklahoma, Missouri, and Florida put more convicted criminals to death than any other states, and they have long been plagued with the highest homicide rates in the country. According to Cassell, it is only rational that they would pursue the death penalty, because they are the ones that need these laws the most. But upon close scrutiny of the murder rate in these southern states, one thing becomes obvious: At the same time that they have aggressively pursued the death penalty over the past decade, their homicide rates have declined—some dramatically. In Oklahoma, for instance, the rate in 1995 was 12.2 murders for every 100,000 people, and by 2007 that number had been slashed in half to 6.1 murders per 100,000. Texas also saw a marked drop in its homicide rate, declining from 9 per 100,000 people in 1995 to 5.9 in 2007. Virginia and Missouri saw double-digit declines in their homicide rates, while Florida's declined from 7.3 in 1995 to 6.6 in 2007. In contrast, North Dakota, which does not have capital punishment legislation in effect, saw a rise in homicide rates from 0.9 per 100,000 people in 1995 to 1.9 in 2007. Wisconsin, Vermont, and Minnesota, 3 other non-death-penalty states, experienced slight decreases in their murder rates over the 12-year period.

So exactly what do these statistics show? If one lumps states together and compares only crime rates and execution rates without taking other factors into consideration such as the size and population of the state, its geographic location, and historic crime trends, it appears that the death penalty does not reduce crime—and in fact, may have the opposite effect. But upon closer examination, it appears that states that have led the country in executions have seen a significant drop in homicide rates over the past few decades. So which is it? Does the death penalty deter crime or not? According to Emory University economist Paul Rubin, the answer largely depends on the personal agendas of those who study capital punishment and have points that they are intent on proving. "Instead of people sitting down and saying 'let's see what the data shows,'" he says, "it's people sitting down and saying 'let's show this is wrong.' Some scientists are out seeking the truth, and some of them have a position they would like to defend."[35]

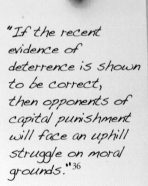

"If the recent evidence of deterrence is shown to be correct, then opponents of capital punishment will face an uphill struggle on moral grounds."[36]

— Cass R. Sunstein and Adrian Vermeule.

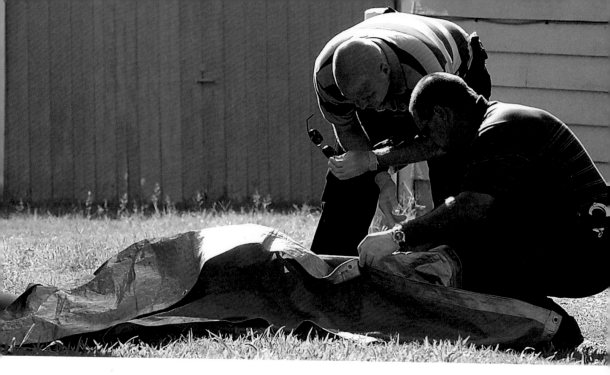

## Inconclusive Evidence

Whether the crime rate is affected positively or negatively because of the death penalty is at the very core of the capital punishment controversy—a controversy that has its roots in centuries of debate and will not likely fade anytime soon. Numerous studies have been done over the years to examine this, from early research by Ehrlich and Layson to more recent studies by Adler, Summers, and others. Still, the issue remains unresolved. There has yet to be one study that conclusively proves, beyond a shadow of a doubt, that the death penalty reduces crime. Nor has there been any study proving that it does not deter crime. According to Sunstein, whether a causal relationship will ever be proved or disproved comes down to the evidence. If one day someone finally succeeds at showing that capital punishment is a certain crime deterrent, those who support it will invariably win their battle to retain execution as the ultimate punishment. In a January 2006 article, Sunstein and coauthor Adrian Vermeule discussed this: "If the recent evidence of deterrence is shown to be correct, then opponents of capital punishment will face an uphill struggle on moral grounds. If each execution is saving lives, the harms of capital punishment would have to be very great to justify its abolition, far greater than most critics have heretofore alleged."[36]

*Police detectives in Oklahoma examine a body at the scene of a suspected double homicide. Oklahoma is one of several states with a large number of executions and a high homicide rate, although the homicide rate was cut in half between 1995 and 2007.*

- With more than 37 million people, California is America's most populous state and has the largest number of death row inmates, but it has executed fewer criminals in recent years than Delaware, with a population of less than 1 million.

- The Death Penalty Information Center says that southern states account for 80 percent of all executions.

- A 2006 study by the University of Houston showed that following an Illinois moratorium on executions during 2000, 150 additional murders were committed over the next 4 years.

- According to professors Cass Sunstein and Justin Wolfers, murder rates in the 12 states that have not executed a prisoner since 1960 are similar to those that subsequently adopted the death penalty.

- Kansas has not executed anyone since 1965, and since that time the state's homicide rate has risen from 2.7 murders per 100,000 people to 3.9 per 100,000.

- The homicide rate in South Dakota, a state that has death penalty legislation in place, is higher than North Dakota, which does not have it.

# Does the Legal Process Hamper the Death Penalty's Deterrence Effect?

**E**ven though Cesare Beccaria was an adamant opponent of the death penalty, in his 1767 essay he discussed the importance of punishment being imposed quickly after a crime was committed. "The more immediately after the commission of a crime a punishment is inflicted, the more just and useful it will be," Beccaria wrote. "An immediate punishment is more useful; because the smaller the interval of time between the punishment and the crime, the stronger and more lasting will be the association of the two ideas of *crime* and *punishment*."[37] Many supporters of capital punishment insist that it would be much more effective as a crime deterrent if criminals were executed shortly after their convictions. Virtually all who are sentenced to die appeal their sentences over and over again, often dragging out their prison terms for years or even decades. Death penalty proponents argue that such delays hamper the cause-and-effect relationship between crime and punishment.

This was the subject of an extensive study published in 2004 by Emory University economics professor Joanna Shepherd. After analyzing monthly murder, execution, and death-row data spanning a period of more than 20 years, Shepherd found that longer waits between the time of sentencing and execution lessened the death penalty's deterrence effect. She explains:

> If criminals prefer lengthy death row waits to short ones, as their numerous appeals and requests for stays suggest, then shortening the time until execution could increase the death penalty's deterrent impact. I find that shorter waits on death row increase deterrence. Specifically, one extra murder is deterred for every 2.75-years reduction in the death-row wait before each execution.[38]

## Appealing a Death Sentence

Shepherd's research findings echo the perspectives of numerous people who think the time between sentencing and execution should be shortened. But even many who support capital punishment say that there are important reasons why the current system is in place and that it is necessary. In a March 9, 2009, ruling, Supreme Court justice John Paul Stevens stated that some people blame the Court's insistence on excessive process for delays in carrying out executions. Stevens writes:

> But delays have multiple causes, including the States' failure to apply constitutionally sufficient procedures at the time of initial [conviction or] sentencing. . . . The reversible error rate in capital trials is staggering. More than 30 percent of death verdicts imposed between 1973 and 2000 have been overturned, and 129 inmates sentenced to death during that time have been exonerated, often more than a decade after they were convicted. Judicial process takes time, but the error rate in capital cases illustrates its necessity. We are duty bound to "insure that every safeguard is observed" when "a defendant's life is at stake."[39]

The appeals process, available to all who are sentenced to die, is long and complex. Although it is mandated by the U.S. Constitution and is upheld by the Supreme Court, the process begins

# A Murderer Who Wanted to Die

On January 16, 2003, after Rocky Barton's wife said she intended to leave him, he was consumed with rage. Later that day, when she went home to collect her belongings, Barton pulled out a shotgun and murdered her in the driveway. He was arrested, and at his trial the following September, the jury found him guilty of aggravated murder. Instead of pleading for leniency, Barton asked them to give him the death penalty. In a 2006 interview with Court TV News, he stated:

> At this time, my attorneys advised me to beg for my life. I can't do that. I strongly believe in the death penalty. And for the ruthless, cold-blooded act that I committed, if I was sitting over there, I'd hold out for the death penalty. . . . Punishment would be to wake up every day and have a date with death. That's the only punishment for this crime. . . . Instead of sitting on death row for 10 or 20 years and having the stress of fighting the legal system, I don't think I could stand it. I can't stand it mentally. So, mainly it's because of guilt for what I done. I feel like I deserve to die.

On July 12, 2006, Barton was executed by lethal injection in Lucasville, Ohio. After spending less than three years in prison, his stint on death row was the shortest in the state's modern history.

Quoted in Emanuella Grinberg, "His Crime: A Farmhouse Ambush and a Suicide Attempt," Court TV News, July 7, 2006. www.courttv.com.

at the state level, and each state has its own procedure in place for handling appeals. In Alabama, for instance, an individual who is convicted of capital murder and given the death penalty is entitled to an automatic appeal that is heard by the Alabama Court of Criminal Appeals. If that effort fails, the case returns to the circuit court where the original trial was held. During that session the defendant's attorney may introduce any issues that were not eligible for presentation during the direct appeal. The court's decision can then be appealed by the defendant to the Alabama Court of Criminal Appeals or to the Alabama Supreme Court. Those appeals are not automatic, however, and both courts have the power to refuse to hear them.

The appeals process in Virginia also begins with an automatic appeal, but it is filed with the state supreme court rather than a court of appeals. The filing includes all papers and physical evidence that were presented during the trial, as well as a written record of all trial testimony. The defense attorney then files a brief arguing that the defendant's conviction and/or death sentence should be reversed because of errors that occurred during the trial. The state attorney general's office responds to the allegations with a brief of its own, and the defendant has the ability to file a reply brief. After all briefs have been filed, the state supreme court schedules the case for oral argument. During the session each side has 30 minutes to discuss what happened in the lower court, but no new evidence or facts may be presented. The time of the oral argument to the supreme court's announcement of its decision is approximately seven weeks. If the court decides in favor of the defendant, the case will go back to trial. If the court's decision is that the conviction should stand, the defendant may appeal to U.S. federal courts.

The first tier of the federal appeals process is the U.S. district court. The defendant files a petition saying that the conviction and/or sentence should be overturned because his or her federal constitutional rights were violated. The state attorney general then responds to the defendant's allegations, arguing that the sentence and conviction should be upheld and explaining why. If that appeal is rejected, the defendant may file a brief with the U.S. court of appeals, again alleging wrongdoing on the part of the district court and asking that the case be reviewed by the higher court. Again, the state attorney general files a reply brief.

"An immediate punishment is more useful; because the smaller the interval of time between the punishment and the crime, the stronger and more lasting will be the association of the two ideas of crime and punishment."[37]

— Cesare Beccaria, in his 1767 essay on crime and punishment.

If the court of appeals effort is unsuccessful, the defendant can file what is known as a writ of certiorari with the U.S. Supreme Court. From a Latin term meaning "to be informed," a writ of certiorari is a formal brief stating that the decision of the court of appeals was incorrect and requesting that the Supreme Court review it. Although the Court has heard many cases, it receives numerous writ of certiorari requests each year, and most are denied. Maryland U.S. district judge Peter J. Messitte explains:

> In recent terms (a term runs from October to June), petitioners have submitted and paid the filing fee in connection with an average of 1,825 petitions. Of these, an average of 80, or roughly 4 percent, have been granted. At the same time, more than 6,000 *in forma pauperis* [in the form of a pauper] petitions (petitions by persons who cannot afford to pay the filing fee, primarily prisoners) have been filed. On average, only five of these are granted annually.[40]

*Forty former death row inmates who appealed their cases and were exonerated of their crimes take part in a conference on wrongful convictions and death sentences. The appeals process is a safeguard but can take years and sometimes even decades.*

Messitte adds that since the 1980s Congress has continued to expand the Supreme Court's power to choose which cases to review. Now the Court has the freedom to make virtually all of its own decisions about cases. Messitte writes:

> Today, using the writ of *certiorari*, the Court considers only cases of "gravity and general importance" involving principles of wide public or governmental interest. . . . Given the Court's inability to hear more than a fraction of the cases for which *cert* is requested, it is not surprising that the justices accept only those raising particularly significant questions of law, and/or those where there is a division of legal authority, as where lower courts have produced conflicting interpretations of constitutional or federal law.[41]

If the Supreme Court turns down a defendant's request to hear a case, all appeals have been exhausted and the execution date is scheduled. The only opportunity left to potentially avoid being put to death is to seek intervention from the state governor. Governors in most states have the power to commute a death sentence to life in prison, an action known as clemency. In Alabama, a defendant whose death sentence has been commuted to life is eligible for parole in 15 years, and this is typical of many states.

## Long Waits on Death Row

The appeals process takes many years to complete, but the amount of time varies. Some states handle their appeals procedures much more quickly than others, which means that appeals to federal courts are expedited. A March 2007 study by Barry Latzer and James N.G. Cauthen of the John Jay College of Criminal Justice in New York examined the appeals procedures of 14 states that have death penalty legislation in place. Latzer and Cauthen concluded that Virginia was the most efficient state at processing appeals, with the time from sentencing to the final state appeal being less than a year. Ohio was found to be the least efficient, with state appeals processes lasting almost 4 years. The entire process, including all state and federal appeals, takes an average of 12.25

years, although many more years often pass before executions take place. The authors of the study write:

> Here is what we already know about overall time consumption in death penalty appeals. Measuring from sentence to execution, it takes more than twelve years to carry out fully reviewed and implemented death sentences in the United States. A substantial number of cases, however, have not completed the review process and the sentence has yet to be carried out. Forty-three percent of those sentenced to death between 1973 and 2005 are still in prison, awaiting the application of the sentence or the resolution of their appeals. At year-end 2005, 339 inmates were under sentence of death for 20 years or more. This is roughly ten percent of the death row population.[42]

Although the time that criminals spend on death row averages about 12 years nationwide, many remain there for decades. California, for instance, has nearly 700 inmates on death row, which is the highest number of all the states. One reason for this is that the time from sentencing to execution is 20 to 25 years, which is nearly twice the national average. According to a June 2008 report by the California Commission on the Fair Administration of Justice, 30 inmates have been on death row more than 25 years, 119 for more than 20, and 240 for more than 15. The state's chief justice, Ronald M. George, testified before the commission and said that if nothing is done, the backlogs in post-conviction proceedings will continue to grow "until the system falls of its own weight."[43]

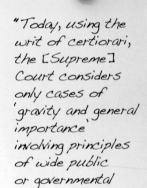

"Today, using the writ of certiorari, the [Supreme] Court considers only cases of 'gravity and general importance' involving principles of wide public or governmental interest."[41]

— U.S. district judge Peter J. Messitte.

People who advocate for swifter executions argue that the appeals process is badly flawed and long delays between sentencing and execution inhibit the death penalty's ability to deter crime. That was one of the conclusions made by Latzer and Cauthen after completing their study. They write:

> The extent to which the death penalty deters crime is a matter of great controversy and is not addressed by this study. We simply assert here that *if* capital punishment

has a deterrent effect over and above life imprisonment, a lengthy implementation process weakens that effect. Deterrence is based on an association of the crime with its attendant punishment, and the passage of time has long been thought to diminish that association. Delays in carrying out death sentences would undermine the deterrent effect of the death penalty by creating in the minds of potential offenders uncertainty about its imposition.[44]

As a result of their in-depth research, Latzer and Cauthen developed recommendations for how the appeals process could be shortened while still maintaining constitutional requirements. "The death penalty appeals process can be administered in a more efficient manner and still ensure fairness to the accused," they write. One of their suggestions is to eliminate review by intermediate courts during the first appeal and instead follow Virginia's process of having the case go directly to the state's highest court. The authors state that when Ohio switched to direct high court review, the state reduced its time expenditure by 25 percent. Another recommendation is to adopt rules or statutes that impose stricter deadlines on all participants in the appeals process. They explain:

> Deadlines work! Those states with statutes or court rules that set reasonable but enforceable deadlines . . . complete the direct appeals process more expeditiously. For example, Virginia . . . has a supreme court rule giving docket preference to death-sentenced cases. Likewise, a Nevada statute provides that decisions in capital appeals must be reached within 150 days from receipt of the record.[45]

## Exonerating the Innocent

Although it may be true that the appeals process could be shortened without compromising constitutional mandates, some argue that it is risky to tamper with it. Alexander Kozinski writes:

> There is a lot to be said, of course, for the proposition that the death penalty ought to be carried out swiftly. But swift justice is hard to come by because the Supreme Court has

constructed a highly complex—and mutually contradictory—series of conditions that must be satisfied before a death sentence can be carried out. On the one hand, there must be individual justice: there can be no mandatory death sentence no matter how heinous the crime. On the other hand, there must be consistent justice: discretion to impose the death penalty must be tightly circumscribed.

*A Washington forensic scientist tests a shirt for traces of semen that may yield DNA. DNA testing, unavailable until the late 1980s, has led to dozens of exonerations in cases involving people sentenced to die.*

But individual justice is inherently inconsistent—different juries reach different results in similar cases. And there are scores of other issues that arise in every criminal case but take on special significance when death is involved.[46]

One of the major reasons why many oppose shortening the appeals process is the possibility that a person could be convicted and executed for a crime that he or she did not commit. There is no way of knowing whether innocent people have been put to death—but it is probable because DNA testing, which has only been used since the late 1980s, has resulted in more than 230 prisoners being exonerated and released. "All these hundreds of DNA exonerations across the country have demonstrated to anyone who's paying attention that there are far more innocent people in prison than anybody could imagine,"[47] says James McCloskey, the founder of an innocence project in New Jersey known as Centurion Ministries. Although DNA testing is not a guaranteed right under the Constitution, most states have laws in place that require post-conviction access to DNA testing, at least in some circumstances. In March 2009 the U.S. Supreme Court agreed to evaluate the issue and make a ruling about whether all those who are imprisoned should have a constitutional right to such testing under federal law.

Curtis McCarty is someone who would likely not be alive today if the appeals process were shortened. In 1986 McCarty was convicted and sentenced to death for the rape and murder of an 18-year-old woman with whom he had been acquainted. His conviction was based solely on the testimony of a police chemist named Joyce Gilchrist, who said that hairs found at the crime scene matched McCarty's—statements that later proved to be fraudulent. In 2002 McCarty's attorneys were able to secure DNA testing on semen recovered from the victim's body, and test results showed that the semen was not McCarty's. After several additional trials and additional DNA evidence that also exonerated McCarty, he was released from prison on May 11, 2007. He had served 21 years in prison, 19 of which were on death row, for a crime he did not commit. "The death penalty system is broken,"

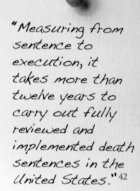

"Measuring from sentence to execution, it takes more than twelve years to carry out fully reviewed and implemented death sentences in the United States."[42]

— Barry Latzer and James N.G. Cauthen of the John Jay College of Criminal Justice in New York.

reads an editorial on the U.S. Law Blog. "128 individuals have been released from death rows nationwide when evidence of their innocence emerged. . . . The story of Curtis McCarty is a story that needs to be told, over and over and over again."[48]

## Are Prolonged Stays on Death Row Unconstitutional?

Like many people who have been sentenced to death, McCarty took advantage of the many appeals that were available to him, and he eventually won and was freed. Virtually all prisoners

*Curtis McCarty testifies during a 2008 Nebraska judiciary committee hearing. McCarty spent 21 years in prison, 19 of which were on death row, before DNA testing exonerated him of rape and murder.*

## A Swift Execution

The decades-long waiting time of prisoners on death row is relatively new in U.S. history. As recently as the 1930s, the tendency to execute convicted criminals swiftly was the norm, with the duration between sentencing and execution often no more than a few weeks. On February 15, 1933, in a botched attempt to assassinate Franklin D. Roosevelt, Italian anarchist Giuseppe Zangara shot 5 people in Miami, Florida, where the president was giving a speech. One of the victims was Chicago mayor Anton Cermak, who was gravely wounded and died less than 3 weeks after being shot. Zangara, whose charge had previously been assault with attempt to kill, was indicted for first-degree murder in the mayor's death. At his trial he showed no remorse for the crime as he pled guilty, and on March 20, 1933, he was executed in the electric chair. The short duration between Zangara's arrest and execution—a mere 32 days—is unheard of in America today.

exercise their rights to such appeals and, in doing so, may extend their time on death row for many years. That is why many people find it ironic that some convicted criminals and/or attorneys protest long stays on death row as cruel and unusual punishment. One who shares that perspective is New American Media editor Earl Ofari Hutchinson, who writes: "The glacially slow appeals process is no consolation for the old men who rot on death rows. They're caught in a legal Catch-22. They don't want to die, and they grab at their every appeal in the desperate hope that a miracle will happen. While they wait and wait, they age faster and suffer more mental and physical ailments than other prisoners."[49] Justice Stevens also believes that long-term stays on death row represent a violation of the Eighth Amendment. Moreover, he is convinced that death sentences that are stretched out for decades cannot possibly have value as a deterrent to crime.

The majority of justices do not share Stevens's view, however. This became apparent during a March 9, 2009, ruling, whereby the Supreme Court denied certiorari to convicted murderer Wil-

*A correctional officer walks past inmates at a crowded Alabama prison. Like members of the general public, U.S. Supreme Court justices have differing views on whether the legal process hampers or enhances the death penalty's deterrence effect.*

lie Thompson. After 32 years on death row, Thompson claimed that the excessive time amounted to cruel and unusual punishment. Stevens and Justice Stephen Breyer agreed that this violated the Eighth Amendment, but the other justices did not, and Thompson's request was denied. Justice Clarence Thomas used strong words to convey his thoughts about the case:

> I remain unaware of any support in the American constitutional tradition or in this Court's precedent for the proposition that a defendant can avail himself of the panoply of appellate and collateral procedures and then complain when his execution is delayed. . . . It makes a mockery of our system of justice . . . for a convicted murderer, who, through his own interminable efforts of delay . . . has secured the almost-indefinite postponement of his sentence, to then claim that the almost indefinite postponement renders his sentence unconstitutional.[50]

"All these hundreds of DNA exonerations across the country have demonstrated to anyone who's paying attention that there are far more innocent people in prison than anybody could imagine."[47]

— James McCloskey, founder of Centurion Ministries in New Jersey.

## Can This Be Resolved?

The issue of whether the complicated, lengthy appeals process in the United States impedes the death penalty's ability to deter crime is as controversial as capital punishment itself. Many death penalty supporters insist that its effectiveness depends on executions being carried out swiftly after someone has been sentenced to death. Others disagree, saying that the long appeals process is necessary in order to ensure that criminals are afforded the rights that are mandated by the Constitution. Also, they argue, if there is any chance that convicted people could be found innocent during the appeals process, lengthier stays on death row could prevent them from being executed. So which perspective is correct? That is a question for which there is no easy answer—a question that will likely remain unresolved for many years, if it is ever resolved at all.

## FACTS

- Texas has accounted for 37 percent of executions in the United States since 1977 and an average of 40 percent since 1997.

- A March 2009 report by the Justice Project analyzed the cases of 39 people from Texas who collectively spent more than 500 years in prison for crimes they did not commit.

- Until February 2008, when the state supreme court ruled the practice unconstitutional, Nebraska remained the only state that executed prisoners in the electric chair.

- According to the Death Penalty Information Center, over 35 percent of death sentences are overturned on appeal.

- An April 2009 report titled *Death Row USA* showed that 98.25 percent of prisoners awaiting execution were male.

# CHAPTER FOUR

# Does Fear of the Death Penalty Deter Would-Be Criminals?

**M**ost people have a natural desire to live and will do everything in their power to keep themselves alive. The same desire holds true for most prisoners on death row, as evidenced by the number who spend years appealing their death sentences. This suggests that fear of execution plays a part in the long waits on death row, but does it have any bearing on whether a person commits murder? Does fear of the death penalty deter crime?

Former Texas police officer Jack Blaisdale (not his real name) says that there is no way to prove, with any certainty, that potential murderers would be dissuaded from committing crimes out of fear of the death penalty. "To put it bluntly," he writes, "there is no one-size-fits-all way of proving that killers consider the possibility of dying before they commit murder." Blaisdale adds, however, that he has personally spoken with criminals who were involved in acts that could have turned into death penalty cases,

> and they wouldn't take that last step that would have put them in the death house. One guy who comes to mind was someone I busted on a dope deal. I was having a conversation with him in jail and I congratulated him on not being stupid enough to pull a gun on us. He looked at

me real serious-like and said, "You know, when I saw you guys I knew I was going away forever, but as long as I'm alive maybe I'll get out someday. If they stick me in the gas chamber, it's done."[51]

Blaisdale says that the man was known for having a virtual arsenal of weapons, but he intentionally avoided any situation that could get him charged with capital murder. Blaisdale explains:

> Prison didn't scare this guy . . . but the gas chamber did. Now does that prove that *everyone* thinks the way he did? Of course not. Does it prove that *most* criminals feel that way? No again. But what it *does* show is that the fear of dying influences *some* would-be criminals to think before they commit murder—and that means fewer people have to die. For me, that's reason enough to keep the death penalty.[52]

The likelihood of someone considering the death penalty before committing a crime seems far-fetched to some, especially in light of federal statistics showing that far more murders are committed in the midst of a heated argument than in the course of robberies, burglaries, or other crimes. The Federal Bureau of Investigation (FBI) reported in 2008 that of the 14,831 homicides committed in the United States during 2007, nearly 4,000 resulted from some type of argument, compared to 924 murders that were related to robbery and 86 that involved burglary.

Daniel P. Doyle, professor of sociology and criminology at the University of Montana, elaborated on this point in testimony before the House Judiciary Committee in March 2007. He stated:

> The potential offender has to be willing and able to engage in a kind of rational calculation, weighing perceived potential risks and benefits. This is simply not a common characteristic of most criminals in general and most murderers in particular. These are people who do not think things through before they do them. They tend to act impulsively, seldom considering the consequences of their actions on themselves or others.[53]

## "The Death Penalty Is a Warning"

Few death penalty supporters believe that fear of execution will prevent all murders, but they do believe it acts as a deterrent to some. Dudley Sharp, founder of the pro-death-penalty group Justice Matters, shares one example of a criminal whose fear of the death penalty influenced his choice of where to commit a crime. A law school professor from New York, Robert Blecker, had interviewed a man who was convicted of homicide. "The murderer robbed and killed drug dealers in Washington DC," writes Sharp, "where he was conscious that there was no death penalty. He specifically did not murder a drug dealer in Virginia because, and only because, he envisioned himself strapped in the electric chair, which he had personally seen many times while imprisoned in Virginia."[54]

Whether fear of the death penalty deters people from committing murder is difficult to prove because of the absence of hard facts. Researchers cannot simply gather reliable statistics showing how many people refrained from killing someone because they feared the death penalty. Nor can they assume that the death penalty did not deter such crimes. The late Louis Pojman, a philosophy professor at West Point Military Academy and a frequent writer on controversial issues, commented on this problem in an essay that was originally published in 1998. In that essay Pojman quoted a judge from New York who once stated: "The death penalty is a warning, just as a lighthouse throwing its beams out to sea. We hear about shipwrecks, but we do not hear about the ships the lighthouse guides safely on their way. We do not have proof of the number of ships it saves, but we do not tear the lighthouse down."[55]

Emory University professor Joanna Shepherd is also of the mindset that the death penalty serves as a warning to would-be murderers and that fear of it deters some criminals. She takes as evidence the fact that so many death row inmates fight execution. She writes: "That many potential perpetrators view execution as worse than life imprisonment confirms why the existence of the death penalty would deter at least a few from committing murder." Shepherd's 2004 study compared

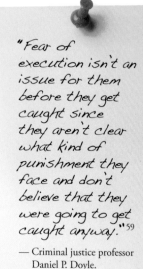

"Fear of execution isn't an issue for them before they get caught since they aren't clear what kind of punishment they face and don't believe that they were going to get caught anyway."[59]

— Criminal justice professor Daniel P. Doyle.

# The Supreme Court's Stance on Fear and the Death Penalty

In its landmark 1972 *Furman v. Georgia* ruling, the U.S. Supreme Court specifically addressed whether the fear of execution deterred potential criminals from committing capital crimes. The Court wrote:

> The available evidence uniformly indicates . . . that the threat of death has no greater deterrent effect than the threat of imprisonment. The States argue, however, that they are entitled to rely upon common human experience, and that experience, they say, supports the conclusion that death must be a more effective deterrent than any less severe punishment. Because people fear death the most, the argument runs, the threat of death must be the greatest deterrent. . . . A rational person contemplating a murder or rape is confronted, not with the certainty of a speedy death, but with the slightest possibility that he will be executed in the distant future. The risk of death is remote and improbable; in contrast, the risk of long-term imprisonment is near and great. In short, whatever the speculative validity of the assumption that the threat of death is a superior deterrent, there is no reason to believe that as currently administered the punishment of death is necessary to deter the commission of capital crimes.

Quoted in FindLaw, "U.S. Supreme Court: *Furman v. Georgia*, 408 U.S. 238 (1972)." http:// caselaw.lp.findlaw.com.

murder rates before and after the Supreme Court's moratorium on capital punishment. She writes: "The before-and-after comparisons reveal that as many as 91 percent of states experienced an increase in murder rates after they suspended the death penalty. In about 70 percent of the cases, the murder rate dropped after the state reinstated the death penalty."[56]

## Crimes of Passion

During her research, Shepherd also discovered that fear of the death penalty deters all kinds of murders, including so-called crimes of passion that are committed impulsively. She explains:

> Some people in the debate on capital punishment's deterrent effect believe that certain types of murder are not deterrable. They claim that murders committed during interpersonal disputes, murders by intimates, or noncontemplated crimes of passion are not intentionally committed and are therefore nondeterrable. . . . To the contrary, I find that the combination of death row sentences and executions deters all types of murders: murders between intimates, acquaintances, and strangers, crime-of-passion murders and murders committed during other felonies. . . . Although the death penalty may not deter all, or even most, crimes of passion, it deters some of them.[57]

*A death row inmate enters a cell block at a South Carolina prison. Some experts believe that fear of execution may act as a deterrent—at least in some instances.*

Many disagree that the death penalty would deter people from committing crimes of passion. These are generally defined as impulsive acts that occur as a result of sudden anger or heartbreak. Those who argue that the fear of execution would not act as a deterrent maintain that these crimes are not planned and so the people who commit them would be unlikely to consider the consequences of their actions ahead of time. A December 2007 editorial in the *Dallas Morning News* makes this point:

> Murder is often a crime of passion, which by definition excludes the faculties of reason. The jealous husband who walks in on his wife and another man is in no position to deliberate rationally on the consequences of killing his rival. The convenience store robber who chooses in a split-second to shoot the clerk has not pondered the potential outcomes of pulling the trigger. People overtaken by rage, panic or drunkenness should be brought to justice, of course, but they are hardly paragons of pure reason, and it's unreasonable to assert that they consider the possibility of a death sentence when committing their crimes.[58]

## "Fear of Execution Isn't an Issue"

Daniel P. Doyle cites another reason that potential offenders would not consider the possible consequences of their crimes: Most people who commit crimes do not believe they will get caught. He refers to studies in which researchers interviewed prison inmates who had been convicted of homicide and found very few who believed they would be caught. Also, few of the prisoners interviewed had an accurate idea of how they would be punished if they did get caught. "Consequently," Doyle writes, "fear of execution isn't an issue for them before they get caught since they aren't clear what kind of punishment they face and don't believe that they were going to get caught anyway."[59]

Doyle adds that criminals are well aware of the statistics showing that few homicides actually result in executions. In 2007, for instance, 14,831 homicides were committed in the United States, but only 42 executions were carried out that same year. This translates to less than $3/10$ of a percent likelihood of a murder resulting in an execution. With only a remote possibility of execution, few would-be criminals would fear this outcome, say Doyle and others who share this view.

## "Cosmic Retribution"

Although it may sound counterintuitive, the idea that people who commit crimes actually consider their chances of getting caught and punished in some manner may not be all that far-fetched. Pojman contended that criminals do think about the threat of execution before committing crimes. He said that even though the evidence for crime deterrence is controversial and often refuted by death penalty opponents, research has shown that people who commit crimes do so on a "cost-benefit" basis. Pojman wrote:

> If he or she estimates the punishment [to be] mild, the crime becomes inversely attractive, and vice versa. The fact that those who are condemned to death do everything in their power to get their sentences postponed or reduced to long-term prison sentences, in the way *lifers* do not, shows that they fear death more than life in prison. The point is this: Imprisonment constitutes one evil, the loss of freedom, but the death penalty imposes a more severe loss.[60]

In arguing that the threat of execution is a crime deterrent, Pojman used an analogy to make his point:

> Imagine that every time someone intentionally killed an innocent person he was immediately struck down by lightning. When mugger Mike slashed his knife into the neck of the elderly pensioner, lightning struck, killing Mike. His fellow muggers witnessed the sequence of events. When burglar Bob pulled his pistol out and shot the bank teller . . . a bolt leveled Bob, his compatriots beholding the spectacle. Soon men with their guns lying next to them were found all across the world in proximity to the corpses of their presumed victims. Do you think that the evidence of cosmic retribution would go unheeded? We can imagine

the murder rate in the United States and everywhere else plummeting. The close correlation between murder and cosmic retribution would serve as a deterrent to would-be murderers.[61]

# When Killing Is Deliberate and Methodical

The one area where crime experts generally agree that fear of execution is not a deterrent is when someone carries out a plan to kill multiple people in a public place. University of Maryland senior research scientist John Lott performed a study with a colleague at the University of Chicago that confirmed that fear of the death penalty does not deter people who commit mass murder. Lott explains: "The vast majority of these killers either commit suicide or are killed at the scene of the crime. The threat of legal punishment, including the death penalty, doesn't really affect their actions since so many of these criminals expect to die in the course of their crime."[62] Criminal justice experts say that these kinds of killers seek power over their victims. They also get a perverse sense of enjoyment over the fame that will inevitably result from massive publicity of their horrific crimes—even if they know that they will not be around to witness it.

A tragic example of this happened on April 16, 2007, at Virginia Polytechnic Institute and State University (Virginia Tech) in Blacksburg, Virginia. Armed with a pistol in one hand and a semiautomatic handgun in the other and wearing a backpack stuffed with ammunition, 23-year-old Seung-Hui Cho moved through the halls of 2 buildings and began firing at random. Several hours later, when the bloody rampage had ended, 27 students and 5 faculty members were dead, and more than 24 others were injured. After committing the worst school massacre in U.S. history, Cho then put a gun to his head and shot himself to death.

Afterward it was discovered that well in advance of the shooting spree, he had prepared a multimedia manifesto, which he sent

"The fact that those who are condemned to death do everything in their power to get their sentences postponed or reduced to long-term prison sentences, in the way lifers do not, shows that they fear death more than life in prison."[60]

— The late Louis Pojman, who was a professor at West Point Military Academy.

*Police carry injured students and staff from Norris Hall following a shooting that left 32 dead and many injured at Virginia Polytechnic Institute and State University in 2007. Experts say the threat of execution is unlikely to influence a person who commits this type of crime.*

to the NBC television network. In his manifesto, Cho made his malevolent intent abundantly clear. Also clear was the fact that Cho was in no way deterred by the threat of Virginia's death penalty legislation, which includes multiple homicides as one of the crimes punishable by execution.

Although there has been a moratorium on the death penalty in New York since 2004, the state still technically has capital punishment legislation on the books—but that did not stop Jiverly Wong from committing a gruesome mass murder in the city of Binghamton on April 3, 2009. Just after 10:00 A.M., Wong drove to the American Civic Association immigrant center and parked his car in front of the rear exit to barricade it so no one could escape. Then, armed with 2 handguns and carrying a satchel that contained extra ammunition and a large hunting knife, he calmly walked around to the front, went through the door, and started shooting. By the time a police SWAT team entered the building, 13 people were dead and 4 were critically wounded. The officers also found Wong dead, killed by his own gun.

Like Cho, Wong had meticulously planned the murderous rampage ahead of time and mailed a package to a television station earlier that morning. It contained his driver's license, a gun permit with his name on it, and three photographs of him posing with guns. Also in the package was a rambling letter in which Wong revealed paranoid thoughts about police. He then made it clear that he was about to embark on a deadly shooting spree. "I am Jiverly Wong shooting the people," he wrote. After making that threat, Wong ended the letter in a bizarre way, apologizing for his broken English and saying, "Have a nice day."[63]

## Should Executions Be Public?

As horrific as mass murders are, they are really quite rare. But when they do happen, the public attitude tends to swing in the direc-

### "It's a Universal Mindset"

In a December 2008 interview with Catholic News Service, Curtis McCarty spoke about the 21 years he spent in prison, 19 of which were on death row. McCarty had been sentenced to death for committing murder, but was released in May 2007 after DNA evidence proved that he was not guilty. He is convinced that capital punishment is always wrong. "It it immoral, first and foremost," he says. "It sounds clichéd because you hear it so often, but you don't teach people that killing people is wrong by killing people. It's illogical and immoral." McCarty also stated his belief that death penalty supporters want to believe it is a deterrent to crime but that is not the case. He explains: "There's not a person alive who does not know what will happen to them if they get caught. People who commit crimes don't think they are going to get caught. It's a universal mindset."[1]

William Moore is another former death row prisoner, and his perspective on capital punishment mirrors that of McCarty. "Getting caught is not part of their plan," he says. "Every criminal I've talked to didn't plan to get caught, so the punishment of the death penalty never comes into the equation."[2]

1. Quoted in Cindy Wooden, "Former Death-Row Inmates Say Death Penalty Immoral, Not a Deterrent," Catholic News Service, December 2, 2008. www.catholicnews.com.
2. Quoted in Wooden, "Former Death-Row Inmates Say Death Penalty Immoral, Not a Deterrent."

tion of favoring the death penalty. This became apparent in a June 2001 *USA Today*/Gallup poll, in which respondents were asked if they supported the execution of Timothy McVeigh. In 1997 he was convicted and sentenced to death for the 1995 bombing of the Alfred P. Murrah Federal Building in Oklahoma City. The blast killed 168 people, including 19 children, and injured 450 others. Of the poll participants who supported the death penalty,

*Rescue workers survey the damage caused by a bomb blast at the Alfred P. Murrah Federal Building in Oklahoma City in 1995. The horrific nature of this crime, which resulted in 168 deaths and 450 injured, reinvigorated the debate over public executions.*

59 percent said he should be executed. Another 22 percent who were *against* capital punishment said he should be executed. This 81 percent in favor of McVeigh's execution is in stark contrast to a poll a month earlier, in which only 52 percent of respondents favored the death penalty for murder.

Another perspective on McVeigh's execution was that it should be televised. In interviews with reporters, he had referred to those who died in the bombing as "collateral damage," stating he felt no remorse for killing them and had no sympathy for the survivors. In response, outraged people throughout the United States called for McVeigh's execution to be televised. Today many people still support public executions, but it is a source of controversy. Since the 1930s, executions in the United States have been held behind closed doors in prison execution rooms. Who is allowed to witness an execution varies from state to state, but in general this includes relatives of the victims and prisoner, prison warden and guards, spiritual advisor(s), and in some cases representatives of the media. Those who support public executions argue that capital punishment would be more of a deterrent if executions were not carried out in private. Rather, they say, let the public watch them, because seeing a convicted murderer put to death might cause would-be criminals to rethink their decisions to kill. That was Pojman's perspective, and he felt strongly about it. "Public executions of the convicted murderer would serve as a reminder that crime does not pay," he wrote. "Public executions of criminals seem an efficient way to communicate the message that if you shed innocent blood, you will pay a high price."[64] Pojman added that he definitely believed such publicity would be a deterrent to homicide.

This point of view found an unusual spokesperson in convicted killer Richard Hinojosa. Hinojosa was put to death in Huntsville, Texas, in August 2006. Before his execution he spoke about his support for allowing the public to witness this event. Hinojosa had been convicted of raping a neighbor and stabbing her to death in 1994. During an interview with Court TV News, Hinojosa was asked about the death penalty as a deterrent to those who might

"The threat of legal punishment, including the death penalty, doesn't really affect their actions since so many of these criminals expect to die in the course of their crime."[62]

— University of Maryland scientist John Lott, speaking of mass murderers.

consider committing murder, and he answered that publicity was the only way it would deter crime. He said:

> I honestly feel that the death penalty, they say it's a deterrent and everything . . . if you're going to use it as a deterrent, it should be done in the public eye. If they're going to do it, they should do it at a time when children are in school and old enough to see this and televise it, so they can see what the outcome of leading a bad life can come to. Children don't even pay attention to what's going on in the news or the papers, so how can it be a deterrent? It's impossible. They should take it to junior high school and have it televised, and say this man's going to be executed. . . . They can put it on time-delay, so they can knock out what [the inmate] is saying. If he's offering good wisdom, why not let the children see it? Especially if they're going down the wrong side of the road and need to be moved back to the right path. . . . When you do it sterile and behind closed doors, it's not a deterrent.[65]

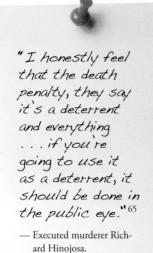

"I honestly feel that the death penalty, they say it's a deterrent and everything . . . if you're going to use it as a deterrent, it should be done in the public eye."[65]

— Executed murderer Richard Hinojosa.

## Fear or No Fear

Whether the fear of execution deters would-be criminals from committing murder is an issue that is an ongoing source of controversy. Studies such as Joanna Shepherd's seem to indicate that this is the case, while other researchers say that there is no evidence to prove it. Blaisdale shares his perspective:

> In short, statistics simply cannot give us the answer. Take, for example, 2004 when there were 400 fewer homicides than in 2003. We know for a fact that the number of murders dropped because FBI crime stats show that they did. But did the drop have anything to do with would-be killers fearing execution? There is absolutely no way to determine that. I firmly believe that the death penalty deters crime. But does it deter one death a year? 600 a year? A thousand? We don't know. We'll never know.[66]

# FACTS

- According to the FBI, nearly half of all murder victims in 2007 were killed by someone they were married to, romantically involved with, related to, or knew.

- The U.S. Bureau of Justice Statistics reports that during 2008, 37 inmates were executed, representing 5 fewer than in 2007.

- As of July 2008 there were 3,307 prisoners on death row in the United States, compared with 517 in 1968.

- The Bureau of Justice Statistics states that the number of prisoners under sentence of death decreased for the sixth consecutive year in 2006.

- Amnesty International reports that although worldwide figures for those currently condemned to death and awaiting execution is difficult to assess, the number is estimated to be between 19,185 and 24,646.

# Are Alternative Punishments More Effective at Deterring Crime?

O n August 24, 2006, Justin Fuller was executed by lethal injection in Huntsville, Texas. Nine years earlier Fuller and three accomplices brutally murdered their neighbor Donald Whittington after spraying him with tear gas, binding and blindfolding him, and then forcing him to withdraw money from an ATM machine. No one knows if Fuller thought about the possibility of a death sentence before he murdered Whittington. But three weeks before his execution, he spoke with a reporter for Court TV News about the death penalty and its deterrent effect. "Killing for killing doesn't solve anything, it doesn't change anything," he said. "People don't think about the death penalty when they go commit crime."[67]

Fuller was not given the option of serving a life sentence, but he expressed equal disdain for spending his life in prison with no chance of release. "To me, life without parole is just another form of the death sentence. Because you're slowly deteriorating . . . you're slowly rotting. You slowly lose the mind frame that you have. . . . So, I don't believe in life without parole."[68] Although Fuller viewed a death sentence and a life sentence as the same, most people, including many death row inmates, do differentiate between the two. And the differences between a death and life sentence are at the very core of the debate over which punishments are most effective at deterring crime.

# Imprisoned for Life

People who commit criminal acts are generally given sentences that fit the severity of the crimes. For instance, nonviolent offenders may be punished by work-release programs, community service, restitution (payment) to victims, or short prison sentences. But for those who commit capital murder, there is only one alternative to the death penalty: life in prison. In some cases, people who have been sentenced to life have been considered rehabilitated and released after serving many years in prison. This is a controversial issue, however, because of the perceived danger they present to society.

The American Civil Liberties Union (ACLU) believes that a life sentence without the possibility of parole may be an even worse punishment than execution because a lifetime in prison can be a grim existence. Prisons in California, for instance, are among the most crowded and violent in the United States. Facilities that were originally designed to hold about 100,000 inmates now house almost 160,000, the *New York Times* wrote in August 2008. Also, an estimated 70 percent of California's prison inmates are affiliated with prison gangs, and this often leads to outbreaks of violence. At Pelican Bay Prison in northern California, which houses more than 1,200 inmates and is known for being a violent facility, assaults, stabbings, and attacks on staff occur on a weekly basis.

The ACLU states:

> Spending even a small amount of time in California's overcrowded, dangerous prisons is not pleasant. Spending thirty years there, growing sick and old, and dying there, is a horrible experience. . . . Prisoners condemned to die in prison are not given any special treatment and, in fact, have less access to programs than other prisoners. They are housed in high security facilities with few privileges, far away from any relatives, and in crowded group cells. Ironically, people on death row are provided much more comfortable single cells and sometimes gain celebrity and attention just by being there.[69]

*"To me, life without parole is just another form of the death sentence. Because you're slowly deteriorating . . . you're slowly rotting."* [68]

— Justin Fuller, a convicted murderer who was executed in August 2006.

Although the deterrent effect is difficult to measure, the ACLU is among those groups and individuals that view a life sentence as a potentially greater crime deterrent than a death sentence.

Some death penalty supporters might even agree with this if they knew that a life sentence without parole actually meant that—in all cases. The reality is that it does not. With a life sentence there is no guarantee that a violent criminal will not someday be released into society. As former police officer Jack Blaisdale writes: "The fact is, NOTHING is forever except the death penalty. . . . As long as fallible systems, people, and whiny do-gooders exist in the world, nothing is forever—that homicidal little maggot who killed a bunch of people is going to be let out someday." Blaisdale admits that he would support life without parole as an alternative if he "thought for one second it was actually going to be applied. I don't, and I never have."[70]

*Guards at San Quentin Prison in California escort a death row inmate from an exercise pen. The state's prisons are among the most crowded and violent in the nation. Some experts believe that the grim existence of a life term provides greater deterrence than a death sentence.*

# Released from Death Row

In fact, 30-plus years ago hundreds of death row inmates actually were released from prisons all across the country. This occurred because of the Supreme Court's official moratorium on executions with its *Furman v. Georgia* ruling in 1972. As a result of the ruling, prisoners who had been condemned to death were resentenced to life in prison without parole—but in the course of fulfilling their prison sentences, many were later granted parole.

Attorney Joan Cheever became interested in the death penalty's deterrence effect after her client, Walter Williams, was executed for murder in October 1994. Cheever found herself wondering if Williams might have turned away from crime if he were given the chance to live and had been rehabilitated while he was incarcerated. This made her curious about whether the same might be true of convicted murderers who escaped the death penalty and were released from prison. Cheever focused on former death row inmates whose sentences were commuted to life in prison after the *Furman v. Georgia* ruling, and she interviewed 322 who had been released. Once her research was completed, she wrote about her findings in the book *Back from the Dead*.

From her research Cheever learned that 111 of the ex-convicts returned to prison—but their crimes were mostly nonviolent offenses such as probation violation or burglary. Only 36 of the 322 returned to prison for more violent offenses: 29 for armed robbery or aggravated assault and 5 for murder. Book reviewer David R. Dow writes: "Most people, I suspect, tend to think that murderers will surely murder again. Cheever's story demonstrates the contrary."[71]

Cheever found that most of the people she interviewed were remorseful about the crimes they had committed. Many of them had struggled with life issues such as holding on to jobs, staying in relationships, and avoiding substance abuse. Others seemed to have adjusted well to their new lives. Dow writes:

> What this book proves, with the cold, hard, unemotional data of laboratory science, is that every year we as a society, if we wanted to, could salvage 40 or 50 people instead of

"Prisons are there for a purpose. There's some fools that need to be there. But there also are inmates worth saving."[73]

—Steven Blackburn, a convicted murderer who spent 12 years in prison.

executing them. For reasons having to do with our own psychological needs, we want to see the people we execute as dangerous rabid animals. Cheever's book unmasks this lie. Her intimate reporting reveals them as human beings—flawed, to be sure, and deserving of punishment, no doubt, but human nonetheless.[72]

## Can Murderers Be Rehabilitated?

Cheever's research shows that a person who has murdered once will not necessarily murder again. Steven Blackburn is an example of this. Blackburn spent 12 years in prison for murder until he was paroled in 1991. He now works as a social worker in Philadelphia and is living proof that some people who commit murder can, with counseling and other assistance, rejoin society. "Prisons are there for a purpose," he says. "There's some fools that need to be there. But there also are inmates worth saving. Other people in prison positively affected my life, so I know it's true."[73]

The prospect of releasing convicted murders back into society does not please many people. They wonder whether the ex-prisoners can ever be trusted, whether they are con artists, and whether they will turn around and commit murder again. Over the years James Hamm has learned to live with that stigma. In 1974 he shot and killed a man during a drug deal that involved an attempted robbery, and along with an accomplice, he shot a second man who also died. To avoid the death penalty, Hamm pled guilty to first-degree murder and was sentenced to life at Arizona State Prison with no eligibility for parole for 25 years. During his incarceration, he spent a lot of time thinking about his life and all the ways he had gone wrong. He earned a college degree in sociology, helped other prisoners learn to read, and wrote numerous grant applications for libraries and for programs for the disabled.

After Hamm was paroled in 1992, he completed law school and passed the bar examination, but because of his criminal record, he was denied the ability to become an attorney. Hamm's

"Of all the government programs in the world that put innocents at risk, is there one with a safer record and with greater protection than the US death penalty? Unlikely."[77]

— Dudley Sharp, founder of the pro-death-penalty group Justice Matters.

critics say that his violent past should preclude him from practicing law, and his efforts to do so have been opposed by several large law firms, the State Bar of Arizona, and the Arizona attorney general, among others. He attempted to get his case before the U.S. Supreme Court, but the justices refused to hear his appeal. A May 2006 article in *American Chronicle* was a scathing rebuke of the movement against him: "The message sent by the U.S. Supreme Court to millions of Americans, as well as to Hamm, is that there is no such thing as rehabilitation for ex-convicts. No matter what you do, no matter what you say, no matter how productive of a human being you become—you will never be rehabilitated."[74] Although Hamm cannot get a license to practice law, he works as a criminal justice consultant and paralegal and is often called upon as an expert witness on various issues related to prisons and the death penalty.

*James Hamm, incarcerated for first-degree murder, turned his life around while in prison. After being paroled, Hamm completed law school and passed the bar exam. He cannot legally practice law but he works as a criminal justice consultant and paralegal.*

## Life in Prison Versus Life Without Parole

Nearly all U.S. states with capital punishment laws reserve the sentence of death for those who have committed capital murder, which generally refers to a crime in which a person intentionally, knowingly, and/or maliciously kills someone. This may be compared to lesser degrees of homicide such as those committed in the course of a robbery or during an argument (a crime of passion). Although those are treated as serious crimes, and often result in lengthy prison terms, they are not considered premeditated or intentional and do not qualify for the death penalty.

Convicted murderers who receive life sentences may be eligible for parole at some point, but it is rarely granted. Parole boards must approve their release, and are often influenced by prosecutors and the families of victims to stop the parole from taking place. Those who are sentenced to life in prison without the possibility of parole only become eligible for release if the governor of their state intervenes on their behalf, or their conviction is overturned by the courts. In 2008 Michigan governor Jennifer Granholm endorsed a parole board recommendation that Dante Ferrazza be released. Ferrazza had been convicted of first-degree murder and sentenced to life in prison with no chance of parole in 1967. He had already spent 42 years in prison and at 71 years of age, Granholm agreed with the board that he no longer posed a threat to society. In February 2009, however, Ferrazza's parole request was denied.

## Killers Who Kill Again

Blackburn and Hamm managed to turn their lives around, but that is not always the outcome. Kenneth Allen McDuff was sentenced to die in the 1960s. McDuff had forced a teenage girl named Edna Sullivan and 2 teenage boys into the trunk of a car. He and an accomplice drove the teens to a secluded spot, where they shot the

2 boys to death and then raped the girl. U.S. district judge Paul Cassell tells what happened next: "McDuff then tortured Sullivan with a soft drink bottle and a broken broom handle, finally killing her by crushing her neck."[75] A jury convicted him and recommended the death penalty, which was imposed by the judge. Then in 1972, during the moratorium on executions, McDuff was resentenced to life in prison.

Authorities granted McDuff parole in 1989—and he promptly went on a vicious killing spree, raping and torturing at least 9 women in Texas. One of McDuff's victims was 28-year-old Colleen Reed; her torture and death were shockingly similar to Sullivan's. McDuff forced Reed into a car, and as his accomplice drove to a secluded spot, McDuff repeatedly raped her in the backseat, and then tortured her with burning cigarettes. "Finally," writes Cassell, "as Reed pleaded for her life, McDuff killed her by crushing her neck." Finally, in 1992 McDuff was arrested, convicted, and again sentenced to death. His execution took place in 1998. "McDuff's torture and slaying of Reed and numerous other women are horrific standing alone," writes Cassell. "But what makes his murders even more tragic is that they were easily preventable. . . . Abolition of the death penalty has its consequences."[76]

Had McDuff been executed in line with his original sentence, these other deaths would not have occurred. Examples such as this lead death penalty supporters to conclude that the only certain deterrence to killers killing again is to put them to death. Dudley Sharp writes:

"A sociopath's mantra: 'Do unto others before they do unto you.'"[78]

— Psychotherapist Juliann Mitchell.

> To state the blatantly clear, living murderers, in prison, after release or escape, are much more likely to harm and murder, again, than are executed murderers. Although an obvious truism, it is surprising how often folks overlook the enhanced incapacitation benefits of the death penalty over incarceration. . . . Of all the government programs in the world that put innocents at risk, is there one with a safer record and with greater protection than the US death penalty? Unlikely.[77]

Many psychologists and criminal justice experts say that murderers such as McDuff are sociopaths, or violent people who have no regard for other human beings or their property and who lack a conscience. Psychotherapist Juliann Mitchell says that this sort of person is incapable of feeling sorrow or sadness for any wrongdoings. They take pleasure in getting away with illegal acts—even feeling a perverse sense of joy at their ability to hurt others. Mitchell says: "To a sociopath, others are always expendable: family, friends, acquaintances. . . . A sociopath's mantra: 'Do unto others before they do unto you.'"[78] Because sociopaths are typically compulsive liars, they have the ability to act like model prisoners so that they will be paroled. This, say death penalty advocates, puts society in danger because these sorts of people have no hesitation about committing murder.

## Violent Gangs in Prisons

Even when violent criminals are locked up for life, it does not guarantee that imprisonment will deter them from committing murder. According to federal crime statistics, the number of inmate-on-inmate homicides doubled from 6 in 2005 to 12 in 2007 and rose to 15 during the first 6 months of 2008. *Boston Globe* columnist Jeff Jacoby says that people often argue that capital punishment is not necessary because convicted murderers can be sentenced to life in prison. He writes: "Lock up even the worst murderers and throw away the key, the theory goes, and they can never kill anyone again. But they can and often do."[79]

A major factor that influences violence inside prison walls is gangs. Criminologists have long known that violent prison gangs such as the Mexican Mafia and Aryan Brotherhood have many members who are on the outside, and they find ways to communicate such as smuggling letters out of the prison. A June 2006 article in the *San Diego Union-Tribune* explains that prison gang members exert their authority over others through violence and threats of violence. "Members and their associates remain loyal to the gang whether in or out of prison. . . . Gang members outside prison have an incentive to cooperate, because if they don't, they risk assault, and they do not want members of their gang inside the prison to be assaulted."[80]

"*I just snapped. I just snapped. I killed her. I killed her.*"[81]

— Enoch Hall, on his stabbing and murder of prison guard Donna Fitzgerald.

*Photographs of neo-Nazi and gang tattoos hang on a wall in the gang unit office of a Southern California police station. Violent gangs such as the Aryan Brotherhood, identified through symbols like these, have orchestrated killings both in and out of prison.*

The article also describes the indictment of 22 members of the Mexican Mafia on charges of running a massive crime syndicate in Southern California. Sixteen of those indicted were already in prison, including Raul Leon, a convicted murderer who was an inmate at Pelican Bay. Leon was accused of being the mastermind behind the syndicate and was charged with ordering murders inside and outside of the prison. Because these violent inmates continuously present such dangerous threats to society, death penalty advocates argue that they should be executed rather than kept in prison.

People who work for prisons are also at risk of being harmed by violent inmates, and this is another argument given in favor of the death penalty. On June 25, 2008, prison guard Donna Fitzgerald was killed by a convict at Tomoka Correctional Institution in Daytona Beach, Florida. Fitzgerald was searching for inmate Enoch Hall, a convicted rapist and kidnapper who had been at the facility since 1994. When Fitzgerald walked into a welding shed and discovered Hall hiding there, she confronted him and he became violent, stabbing her in the back multiple times with a knife that he had made out of sheet metal. Fitzgerald died after the brutal stabbing, and Hall was charged with first-degree murder. "I just snapped. I just snapped. I killed her. I killed her,"[81] Hall told corrections officers just before they found Fitzgerald's body slumped over a pushcart. Florida is a

## Making Prisons Safer

If convicted murderers are sentenced to life in prison without parole, many people believe that is sufficient punishment. They maintain that executing such prisoners is unnecessary because they will never be part of society again. But even if these convicts are locked up forever, that does not necessarily mean they will refrain from committing criminal acts. Prisons can be dangerous places where violence is a regular occurrence, and the lives of inmates and guards are constantly at risk. *USA Today*'s Alan Gomez writes: "As recently as 1980, the murder rate in prison was nearly five times as great as in the general population." To address this dire situation, corrections officers throughout the United States are taking measures to make their prisons safer. One of the major changes that has taken place is separating known gang members from other prisoners and putting them into solitary confinement. Texas correctional institutions began doing this in the mid-1980s, and prisons have seen a marked drop in murders since then. In New York, prison officials have begun screening inmates for mental problems and offering group therapy programs and anger management classes. This, too, has led to a significant drop in the number of prison murders.

Alan Gomez, "States Make Prisons Far Less Deadly," *USA Today*, August 23, 2008. www.correctionsone.com.

capital punishment state, and prosecutors declared that they planned to pursue the death penalty for Hall.

## No Simple Answers

Whether convicted murderers should be put to death or punished in alternative ways is an extremely difficult, complex issue to resolve. Death penalty supporters insist that the risk of repeat murders is simply too great for such chances to be taken and that violent criminals must be removed from society permanently by execution. This, they say, is the only way to guarantee that the criminals will be deterred from killing again. Those who believe that rehabilitation can turn even murderers' lives around say that putting them to death accomplishes nothing and is unconscionable. The people whose views fall somewhere in the middle believe that convicted murderers should not be put to death but should spend their entire lives in prison with no chance of parole. Those who have that viewpoint, such as the ACLU, maintain that life without parole is a more effective punishment because prison is such a dismal environment. So will these people who harbor such radically diverse viewpoints ever arrive at a consensus? Even the world's most learned scholars could not possibly predict the answer to that question—nor would they attempt to do so.

## FACTS

- An estimated 8 percent of prisoners currently on death row were previously convicted of homicide before committing the murder that earned them the death penalty.

- A July 2008 poll by Quinnipiac University showed that 47 percent of respondents preferred the death penalty for criminals convicted of murder, 44 percent preferred life in prison with no chance of parole, and 9 percent were unsure.

- A three-year program by the U. S. Department of Labor called Ready4Work provides career mentoring to prisoners, and since it was implemented in 2003, it has been shown to reduce repeat crimes by 50 percent.

- During his first two years in office, Governor Arnold Schwarzenegger paroled 89 convicted murderers.

- A study published in January 2007 by Washington State researchers showed that the risk of death within two weeks after release from prison is 12.7 times higher for former inmates compared to other state residents, with the leading causes being drug overdose, cardiovascular disease, homicide, and suicide.

# Related Organizations

### American Civil Liberties Union (ACLU)
125 Broad St., 18th Floor
New York, NY 10004
phone: (212) 549-2500
fax: (212) 549-2646
e-mail: aclu@aclu.org
Web site: www.aclu.org

The ACLU, which refers to itself as the "nation's guardian of liberty," works with courts, legislatures, and communities to ensure that everyone in the United States is afforded the rights and liberties guaranteed by the Constitution. Its Web site has a death penalty link that features a number of fact sheets, publications, legislative developments, Supreme Court cases, and news releases.

### Amnesty International
1 Easton St.
London
WC1X 0DW, UK
phone: +44-20-74135500
fax: +44-20-79561157
Web site: www.amnesty.org

Amnesty International seeks to stop the abuse of human rights for people worldwide through campaigning and international solidarity. Its Web site offers death penalty reports as well as news articles and a variety of other publications.

### Criminal Justice Legal Foundation (CJLF)
PO Box 1199
Sacramento, CA 95812

phone: (916) 446-0345
Web site: www.cjlf.org

The CJLF is dedicated to restoring a balance between the rights of crime victims and the criminally accused. Its Web site features a number of publications about the death penalty as well as news releases, cases, and Supreme Court decisions.

## Death Penalty Information Center (DPIC)

1101 Vermont Ave. NW, Suite 701
Washington, DC 20005
phone: (202) 289-2275
fax: (202) 289-7336
e-mail: dpic@deathpenaltyinfo.org
Web site: www.deathpenaltyinfo.org

The DPIC, which aims to be a balanced source of information about the pros and cons of the death penalty, serves the media and the public with analyses and information on issues concerning capital punishment. Its Web site, which has been referred to as one of the most comprehensive resources for information on the death penalty, features numerous reports, articles, testimonies, key issues, and fact sheets.

## Equal Justice Initiative

122 Commerce St.
Montgomery, AL 36104
phone: (334) 269-1803
fax: (334) 269-1806
e-mail: contact_us@eji.org
Web site: www.eji.org

The Equal Justice Initiative provides legal representation to indigent defendants and prisoners who have been denied fair and just treatment in the legal system. Its Web site features news articles, information about wrongful convictions, and other publications.

## Innocence Project

100 Fifth Ave., 3rd Floor
New York, NY 10011
phone: (212) 364-5340

e-mail: info@innocenceproject.org
Web site: www.innocenceproject.org

The Innocence Project is dedicated to exonerating wrongfully convicted people through DNA testing and reforming the criminal justice system to prevent future injustice. Its Web site features a number of publications such as news releases, fact sheets, wrongful convictions and exonerations by state, and a quarterly newsletter.

### Justice For All

9525 Katy Freeway
Houston, TX 77024
phone: (713) 935-9300
e-mail: info@jfa.net
Web site: www.jfa.net

Justice For All is a pro-death-penalty organization that seeks change in what it perceives to be a criminal justice system that does not adequately protect the lives and property of law-abiding citizens. Its Web site offers information about criminal executions, a "Victims Voices" section, and other publications related to capital punishment.

### Justice Policy Institute

1003 K St. NW, Suite 500
Washington, DC 20001
phone: (202) 558-7974
e-mail: info@justicepolicy.org
Web site: www.justicepolicy.org

The Justice Policy Institute's mission is to promote effective solutions to social problems and to be dedicated to ending society's reliance on incarceration. Its Web site features news releases, research papers, a quarterly newsletter, and numerous downloadable brochures.

### U.S. Bureau of Justice Statistics

810 Seventh St. NW
Washington, DC 20531
phone: (202) 307-0765

e-mail: askbjs@usdoj.gov
Web site: www.ojp.gov/bjs

The Bureau of Justice Statistics is the United States' primary source for criminal justice statistics. Its Web site links to numerous publications and news releases related to crime, the justice system, courts and sentencing, homicide trends, and the FBI's yearly Uniform Crime Reports.

## U.S. Department of Justice

950 Pennsylvania Ave. NW
Washington, DC 20530-0001
phone: (202) 514-2000
e-mail: askdoj@usdoj.gov
Web site: www.usdoj.gov

The mission of the Department of Justice is to enforce U.S. law, ensure public safety against foreign and domestic threats, provide federal leadership in preventing and controlling crime, seek just punishment for those guilty of unlawful behavior, and ensure fair and impartial administration of justice for all Americans. A wealth of information on the death penalty and related issues may be accessed by using the Web site's search engine.

# For Further Research

## Books

Frank R. Baumgartner, Suzanna L. De Boef, and Amber E. Boydstun, *The Decline of the Death Penalty and the Discovery of Innocence*. New York: Cambridge University Press, 2008.

Hugo Bedau and Paul Cassell, eds., *Debating the Death Penalty*. New York: Oxford University Press, 2004.

Michelangelo Delfino and Mary E. Day, *Death Penalty USA: 2005–2006*. Tampa, FL: MoBeta, 2008.

Rudolph J. Gerber and John M. Johnson, *The Top Ten Death Penalty Myths*. Westport, CT: Praeger, 2007.

Ron Gleason, Desta Garrett, and Ron Kirk, *The Death Penalty on Trial: Taking a Life for a Life Taken*. Ventura, CA: Nordskog, 2009.

Charles S. Lanier, William J. Bowers, and James R. Acker, *The Future of America's Death Penalty*. Durham, NC: Carolina Academic Press, 2008.

Billy Wayne Sinclair and Jodie Sinclair, *Capital Punishment: An Indictment by a Death-Row Survivor*. New York: Arcade, 2009.

Scott E. Sundby, *A Life and Death Decision: A Jury Weighs the Death Penalty*. New York: Palgrave Macmillan, 2005.

## Periodicals

Christian Nolan, "Locking Up Teens Forever," *Connecticut Law Tribune*, December 1, 2008.

Kevin B. O'Reilly, "Doctor Quits Prison Job over Execution," *American Medical News*, February 9, 2009.

Alyson M. Palmer, "DA Vents on Georgia Death Case," *Recorder*, October 16, 2008.

Norm Pattis, "Death Penalty Weighs on Legal System's Soul," *Connecticut Law Tribune*, April 6, 2009.

Leo Strupczewski, "Justices Blast Ex-Judge for Shoddy Work in Capital Case," *Legal Intelligencer*, March 23, 2009.

## Internet Sources

*Dallas Morning News*, "The Myth of Deterrence: Death Penalty Does Not Reduce Homicide Rate," December 2, 2007. www.dallasnews.com/sharedcontent/dws/dn/opinion/editorials/stories/DN-deterrence_1202edi.ART.State.Edition1.36bbe2f.html.

John J. Donohue and Justin Wolfers, "The Death Penalty: No Evidence for Deterrence," *Economists' Voice*, April 2006. www.deathpenaltyinfo.org/DonohueDeter.pdf.

Adam Liptak, "Does Death Penalty Save Lives? A New Debate, *New York Times,* November 18, 2007. www.nytimes.com/2007/11/18/us/18deter.html?pagewanted=1&_r=2.

John Lott, "Death as Deterrent," Fox News, June 20, 2007. www.foxnews.com/story/0,2933,284336,00.html.

Scott Smith, "Death Row Inmates Often Wait Indefinitely for Execution," *Record*, March 7, 2007. www.recordnet.com/apps/pbcs.dll/article?AID=/20070307/A_NEWS/703070336.

Cass R. Sunstein and Justin Wolfers, "A Death Penalty Puzzle," *Washington Post*, June 30, 2008. www.washingtonpost.com/wp-dyn/content/article/2008/06/29/AR2008062901476.html.

Pauline Vu, "Executions Halted as Doctors Balk," *Stateline*, March 21, 2007. www.stateline.org/live/details/story?contentId=190836.

*Washington Times*, "Editorial: Cheapening the Death Penalty," February 27, 2009. www.washingtontimes.com/news/2009/feb/27/cheapening-the-death-penalty.

# Web Sites

**Clark County Prosecuting Attorney** (www.clarkprosecutor.org/html/links/dplinks.htm). Although this site was created by a prosecutor in Clark County, Indiana, it contains an extensive collection of detailed information about executions that have taken place all over the United States.

**Death Penalty Pro/Con** (http://deathpenalty.procon.org). This site provides a balanced look at the death penalty controversy and offers numerous facts, laws, cases, deterrence information, and pro/con statements on questions related to capital punishment.

***The Execution*, PBS Frontline** (www.pbs.org/wgbh/pages/frontline/shows/execution). An excellent and comprehensive inside story of capital punishment and everyone who is involved in any way, from convicted criminals to prison wardens, chaplains, and executioners.

**How Stuff Works** (www.howstuffworks.com). Two articles related to capital punishment appear on this site: "How Lethal Injection Works" and "How Does Death by Hanging Work?" Both are interesting and informative.

**Justia Supreme Court Center** (http://supreme.justia.com). By using this site's search engine, all Supreme Court decisions can be researched, including those that addressed the constitutionality of the death penalty.

**Pro-Death Penalty.com** (www.prodeathpenalty.com). This Web site seeks to inform the public about important issues related to the death penalty, including its deterrent effects, legislation, scheduled executions, and the rights of victims.

# Source Notes

## Introduction: "Something Is Wrong with Their Reasoning"

1. Quoted in Phil Gasper, "Live from Death Row: An Interview with Stanley Tookie Williams," *Monthly Review*, November 28, 2005. http://mrzine.monthlyreview.org.

2. Joseph Farah, "Fry Tookie," *World Net Daily*, November 28, 2005. www.wnd.com.

3. Hugh Bedau and Paul Cassell, eds., *Debating the Death Penalty*. New York: Oxford University Press, 2004, p. 191.

4. Richard Posner, "Further Comments on Capital Punishment: BECKER," The Becker-Posner Blog, December 25, 2005. www.becker-posner-blog.com.

## Chapter One: What Are the Origins of the Death Penalty Controversy?

5. Quoted in Philip English Mackey, *Voices Against Death*. New York: Burt Franklin, 1976, p. 2.

6. Quoted in James J. Megivern, *The Death Penalty: An Historical and Theological Survey*. New York: Paulist, 1997, p. 220.

7. Quoted in Constitution Society, "Of Crimes and Punishments: Cesare Beccaria." www.constitution.org.

8. Quoted in Constitution Society, "Of Crimes and Punishments."

9. Quoted in Constitution Society, "Of Crimes and Punishments."

10. Gary P. Gershman, *Death Penalty on Trial*. Santa Barbara, CA: ABC-CLIO, 2005, p. 28.

11. Cynthia Crossen, "Use of Death Penalty over Decades Points to Conflicted Public," *Wall Street Journal*, May 7, 2007, p. B1.

12. Mackey, *Voices Against Death*, p. xlii.

13. Death Penalty Information Center, "Introduction to the Death Penalty." www.deathpenaltyinfo.org.

14. Quoted in Justia Supreme Court Center, "*Louisiana ex rel. Francis v. Resweber,* 329 U.S. 459 (1947)." http://supreme.justia.com.

15. Quoted in Bedau and Cassell, *Debating the Death Penalty*, p. 23.

16. Quoted in Cornell University Law School, "*Witherspoon v. Illinois* (No. 1,015)." www.law.cornell.edu.

17. Quoted in FindLaw, "U.S. Supreme Court: *Furman v. Georgia,* 408 U.S. 238 (1972)." http://caselaw.lp.findlaw.com.

18. Death Penalty Information Center, "Introduction to the Death Penalty."

### Chapter Two: How Do Executions Affect the Crime Rate?

19. Jeanne Woodford, "Death Row Realism," *Los Angeles Times*, October 2, 2008. www.latimes.com.

20. Woodford, "Death Row Realism."

21. Isaac Ehrlich, "The Deterrent Effect of Capital Punishment: A Question of Life and Death," *American Economic Review*, June 1975. http://wings.buffalo.edu.

22. Jeffrey Fagan, "Deterrence and the Death Penalty: A Critical Review of New Evidence," testimony to the New York State Assembly Standing Committee on Codes, Assembly Standing Committee on Judiciary and Assembly Standing Committee on Correction, January 21, 2005. www.deathpenaltyinfo.org.

23. Quoted in William F. Buckley Jr., "Michael Ross Dead?" *National Review*, January 11, 2005. www.nationalreview.com.

24. Cass R. Sunstein and Justin Wolfers, "A Death Penalty Puzzle," *Washington Post*, June 30, 2008. www.washingtonpost.com.

25. Emma Schwartz, "Crime Rates Shown to Be Falling," *U.S. News & World Report*, June 11, 2008. www.usnews.com.

26. John J. Donohue and Justin Wolfers, "Uses and Abuses of Empirical Evidence in the Death Penalty Debate," *Stanford Law Review*, January 9, 2006. http://bpp.wharton.upenn.edu.

27. Donohue and Wolfers, "Uses and Abuses of Empirical Evidence in the Death Penalty Debate."

28. Donohue and Wolfers, "Uses and Abuses of Empirical Evidence in the Death Penalty Debate."

29. Quoted in Robert Tanner, "Studies Say Death Penalty Deters Crime," *Washington Post*, June 11, 2007. www.washington post.com.

30. Quoted in Tanner, "Studies Say Death Penalty Deters Crime."

31. Quoted in Michael Smerconish, "Death Penalty Deters," *Huffington Post*, November 11, 2007. www.huffingtonpost.com.

32. Sunstein and Wolfers, "A Death Penalty Puzzle."

33. Bedau and Cassell, *Debating the Death Penalty*, p. 192.

34. John Lott, "Death as Deterrent," Fox News, June 20, 2007. www.foxnews.com.

35. Quoted in Fox News, "Studies: Death Penalty Discourages Crime," June 11, 2007. www.foxnews.com.

36. Cass R. Sunstein and Adrian Vermeule, "Is Capital Punishment Morally Required? The Relevance of Life-Life Tradeoffs," Working Paper No. 05-06, AEI–Brookings Joint Center for Regulatory Studies, March 2005, p. 42.

## Chapter Three: Does the Legal Process Hamper the Death Penalty's Deterrence Effect?

37. Quoted in Constitution Society, "Of Crimes and Punishments."

38. Joanna Shepherd, "Capital Punishment and the Deterrence of Crime," written testimony for the House Judiciary Committee, Subcommittee on Crime, Terrorism, and Homeland Security, April 21, 2004. http://judiciary.house.gov.

39. Quoted in Supreme Court of the United States, *William Lee Thompson v. Walter A. McNeil*, March 9, 2009. www.supreme courtus.gov.

40. Peter J. Messitte, "The Writ of Certiorari: Deciding Which Cases to Review," U.S. Department of State's Bureau of International Information Programs, July 29, 2008. www.america.gov.

41. Messitte, "The Writ of Certiorari."

42. Barry Latzer and James N.G. Cauthen, *Justice Delayed? Time Consumption in Court Appeals: A Multistate Study*, Criminal Justice Legal Foundation, March 2007. www.cjlf.org.

43. Quoted in California Commission on the Fair Administration of Justice, *Report and Recommendations on the Administration of the Death Penalty in California*, June 30, 2008. www.ccfaj.org.

44. Latzer and Cauthen, *Justice Delayed? Time Consumption in Court Appeals*.

45. Latzer and Cauthen, *Justice Delayed? Time Consumption in Court Appeals*.

46. Quoted in Bedau and Cassell, *Debating the Death Penalty*, p. 10.

47. Quoted in John Eligon, "New Efforts Focus on Exonerating Prisoners in Cases Without DNA Evidence," *New York Times*, February 7, 2009. www.nytimes.com.

48. U.S. Law Blog, "Curtis McCarty Speaks in Knoxville," April 30, 2008. http://tcask.blogspot.com.

49. Earl Ofari Hutchinson, "Dead Man Wheeled In—the Graying of Death Row," New American Media, January 13, 2006. http://news.pacificnews.org.

50. Quoted in Supreme Court of the United States, *William Lee Thompson v. Walter A. McNeil.*

## Chapter Four: Does Fear of the Death Penalty Deter Would-Be Criminals?

51. Jack Blaisdale, interview with the author, February 25, 2009.

52. Blaisdale, interview.

53. Daniel P. Doyle, "Testimony of Daniel P. Doyle, Ph.D.," House Judiciary Committee, March 9, 2007. http://data.opi.mt.gov.

54. Dudley Sharp, "Cost Savings: The Death Penalty," comment in Bruce Tomaso, "New Mexico Lawmakers Vote to End Death Penalty," *Dallas Morning News* Religion Blog, March 14, 2009. http://religionblog.dallasnews.com.

55. Quoted in Bedau and Cassell, *Debating the Death Penalty*, p. 63.

56. Shepherd, "Capital Punishment and the Deterrence of Crime."

57. Shepherd, "Capital Punishment and the Deterrence of Crime."

58. *Dallas Morning News*, "The Myth of Deterrence: Death Penalty Does Not Reduce Homicide Rate," editorial, December 2, 2007. www.dallasnews.com.

59. Doyle, "Testimony of Daniel P. Doyle, Ph.D."

60. Quoted in Bedau and Cassell, *Debating the Death Penalty*, p. 61.

61. Quoted in Bedau and Cassell, *Debating the Death Penalty*, pp. 58–59.

62. John Lott, "Death as Deterrent."

63. Quoted in Joe Kemp and Corky Siemaszko, "Letter from Jiverly Wong, the Gunman in the Binghamton Massacre, Shows Insight into Paranoid Mind," *New York Daily News*, April 6, 2009. www.nydailynews.com.

64. Quoted in Bedau and Cassell, *Debating the Death Penalty*, p. 59.

65. Quoted in Clark County Prosecuting Attorney, "Richard Hinojosa: Court TV: An Interview with Richard Hinojosa," August 2, 2006. www.clarkprosecutor.org.

66. Blaisdale, interview.

## Chapter Five: Are Alternative Punishments More Effective at Deterring Crime?

67. Quoted in Clark County Prosecuting Attorney, "Justin Chaz Fuller: Court TV," August 2, 2006. www.clarkprosecutor.org.

68. Quoted in Clark County Prosecuting Attorney, "Justin Chaz Fuller."

69. American Civil Liberties Union of Northern California, "The Truth About Life Without Parole: Condemned to Die in Prison." www.aclunc.org.

70. Blaisdale, interview.

71. David R. Dow, "Will Murderers Kill Again?" *Houston Chronicle*, August 10, 2006. www.chron.com.

72. Dow, "Will Murderers Kill Again?"

73. Quoted in Milan Simonich, "Murder's Stain: Can It Be Erased?" *Arizona Bar Review,* August 10, 2003. www.legaled.com/killer.htm.

74. Randy L. Harrington, "Proof That Rhetoric About Prison Rehabilitation Is a Lie," *American Chronicle*, May 31, 2006. www.americanchronicle.com.

75. Bedau and Cassell, *Debating the Death Penalty*, p. 185.

76. Bedau and Cassell, *Debating the Death Penalty*, p. 185.

77. Sharp, "Cost Savings."

78. Juliann Mitchell, "Casey Anthony: Profile of a Sociopath," Blogcritics Culture, October 19, 2008. http://blogcritics.org.

79. Jeff Jacoby, "The Fallacy of Life in Prison," *Boston Globe,* February 8, 2006. http://www.boston.com.

80. Onell R. Soto, "Twenty-two Members of Mexican Mafia Prison Gang Indicted for Racketeering," *San Diego Union-Tribune*, June 16, 2006. www.signonsandiego.com.

81. Quoted in Lyda Longa, "Hall Pleads Not Guilty to Murder," *Daytona Beach News-Journal*, July 18, 2008. www.news-journalonline.com.

# Index

Adler, Roy D., 33
Alabama, appeals process in, 41–42
*American Chronicle* (magazine), 73
American Civil Liberties Union (ACLU), 69
*American Economic Review* (journal), 27
Amnesty International, 24, 67
anti-death penalty movement, 11–12
    early influences on, 12–14
appeals process, 40–44
    length of, 44–45
    percentage of death sentences
        overturned in, 53
    shortening
        dangers of, 46–48
    recommendations for, 46
Arouet, François-Marie. *See* Voltaire

*Back from the Dead* (Cheever), 71
Barton, Rocky, 41
Beccaria, Cesare, 12–14, 39
Berk, Richard, 31
Blackburn, Steven, 72, 74
Blaisdale, Jack, 54–55, 66, 70
Breyer, Stephen, 52
Bureau of Justice Statistics, U.S., 67

Cahn, Edmond, 17
California
    executions in, 38
    number of inmates on death row in, 6, 45
California Commission on the Fair
    Administration of Justice, 45
Canada, crime/death penalty in, vs. in
    U.S., 31–32
Cassell, Paul G., 7–8, 28, 29, 35, 36, 75
Cauthen, James N.G., 44, 45–46
Cermak, Anton, 50

certiorari, writ of, 43
Cheever, Joan, 71, 72
Cho, Seung-Hui, 61–62
Constitution, U.S., *See* Eighth
    Amendment; Fourteenth Amendment;
    Eighteenth Amendment.
crime, Prohibition and increase in, 16–17
Crossen, Cynthia, 16

*Dallas Morning News* (newspaper), 59
death, risk of, for former inmates after
    release from prison, 79
death penalty
    as cosmic retribution, 60–61
    cost of, 26–27
    European views of, 15
    federal, 10
    in history, 11
    1972 moratorium on, 20–24
    nineteenth century reforms in, 14–15
    in other countries, 24
    ruled unconstitutional for rape cases, 25
    states with, 23 (map)
    statistics on crime rates and, 31
    Supreme Court rulings on, 18–24
    twentieth century changes in, 15–17
    U.S. public opinion on, 17, 24
    as warning to potential murderers, 56–58
Death Penalty Information Center, 17, 34, 38
    on percentage of death sentences
        overturned on appeal, 53
death row
    constitutionality of long stays on, 49–54
    inmates on
        average time spent on death row, 44–45

percent having been convicted after a
previous homicide conviction, 79
population on, 67
globally, 67
percent represented by males, 53
*Death Row USA,* 53
death sentences
appeals of, 40–44
decline in number of prisoners under, 67
percent overturned on appeal, 53
decency, evolving standards of, 19
Department of Justice, U.S., 10, 34
Department of Labor, U.S., 79
deterrence
to homicides, capital punishment as, 27–28, 60–61
challenge of interpreting statistics on, 27–2831
life without parole as, 70
to mass murders, death penalty is not effective as, 61–63
types of, 7–8
would be increased with faster executions, 39–40
*The Deterrent Effect of Capital Punishment* (Ehrlich), 27–28
DNA testing, 48
exonerations from, 52, 63
Donohue, John J., 30–32
Dow, David R., 71–72
Doyle, Daniel P., 55, 59–60

Ehrlich, Isaac, 27–28, 34, 37
Eighteenth Amendment, 16
Eighth Amendment, 18
evolving standards of decency contained in, 19
long-term stays on death row as violation of, 50, 52
electric chair, 18, 21, 25, 53
is ruled unconstitutional, 53
execution(s)
fear of, does not deter homicides, 59–60
length of time between conviction and, 44–46
may increase murder rate, 34
numbers of, in U.S., during 1930s, 17
public, 65–66
states leading in, have higher crime rates, 35–36, 38

Fagan, Jeffrey, 27
Farah, Joseph, 7
Federal Bureau of Investigation (FBI), 55
Ferrazza, Dante, 74
Fitzgerald, Donna, 77
Fourteenth Amendment, 21, 22
*Francis v. Resweber* (1946), 18–19
Fuller, Justin, 68
*Furman v. Georgia* (1972), 20–22, 71

gangs, prison, 76–78
George, Ronald M., 45
Georgia, constitutionality of death penalty in, 20–22
Gershman, Gary P., 16
Gilmore, Gary, 25
Gomez, Alan, 78
Granholm, Jennifer, 74
*Gregg v. Georgia* (1976), 23–24, 27

Hall, Enoch, 77–78
Hamm, James, 72–73, 74
Hinojosa, Richard, 65–66
homicides/homicide rate
death penalty deters, 27–28, 32–34
in U.S. vs. Europe, 25
many factors affect, 29–32, 34
numbers of, and executions, in 2007, 59
percent of victims knowing killer, 67
percent related to anger vs. to robbery/burglary, 55
in prisons, 78
Hutchinson, Earl Ofari, 50

Jacoby, Jeff, 76
Jefferson, Thomas, 14
jurors, views on death penalty and exclusion of, 20
Justice Matters, 56
Justice Project, 53

Kansas, murder rate in, 38
Koestler, Arthur, 17
Kozinski, Alexander, 19–20, 46–47
Krisberg, Barry, 34

Latzer, Barry, 44, 45–46
Layson, Stephen, 28, 29, 37
life without parole, 68, 74
death penalty vs., survey on, 79

as less expensive than death penalty, 26–27

as worse sentence than death, 69

Lott, John, 35, 61

Mackey, Philip English, 17

Markman, Stephen, 28, 29

McCarty, Curtis, 48–49, 63

McCloskey, James, 48

McDuff, Kenneth Allen, 74–75, 76

McVeigh, Timothy, 64–65

Messitte, Peter J., 43–44

Mitchell, Juliann, 76

Mocan, Naci, 32–33

Moore, William, 63

National Academy of Sciences, 28

Ohio, appeals process in, 44

opinion polls. *See* surveys

parole, of former death row inmates, 71–72

Pojman, Louis, 56, 60, 65

polls. *See* surveys

Posner, Richard, 9

prison gangs, 76–78

Progressive Era, 15–16

Prohibition, 16

Ready4Work program, 79

Reed, Colleen, 75

*Reflections on Hanging* (Koestler), 17

rehabilitation, 72–73

Roosevelt, Franklin D., 50

Royal Commission on Capital Punishment (U.K.), 17

Rush, Benjamin, 11–12, 14

*San Diego Union-Tribune* (newspaper), 76

Schwartz, Emma, 30

Schwarzenegger, Arnold, 79

Sharp, Dudley, 56, 75

Shepherd, Joanna, 39–40, 56–58

*Southern Economic Journal,* 28

states

with death penalty, 23 (map)

leading in executions have higher crime rates, 34–36

number with death penalty, 24

variation in appeal processes in, 41–42

Stevens, John Paul, 40, 50–51, 52

Sullivan, Edna, 74–75

Summers, Michael, 33, 37

Sunstein, Cass R., 29–30, 35, 37, 38

Supreme Court

issues moratorium on death penalty, 20–24

process of bringing appeals to, 43–44

rulings on death penalty, 18–19

surveys

on death penalty, 24

on death penalty as deterrent, 25

of Europeans, on death penalty as deterrent, 15

on execution of Timothy McVeigh, 64–65

on life without parole vs. death penalty, 79

Texas, executions in, 53

Thomas, Clarence, 52

Thompson, William, 51–52

United States, crime/death penalty in, vs. in Canada, 31–32

*U.S. News and World Report* (magazine), 30

Vermeule, Adrian, 37

Virginia, appeals process in, 42, 44

Virginia Tech shootings (2007), 61–62

Voltaire (François-Marie Arouet), 12

Warren, Earl, 19

Whittington, Donald, 68

Williams, Stanley "Tookie," 6–8

Williams, Walter, 71

*Witherspoon v. Illinois* (1968), 20

Wojtowicz, John, 8

Wolfers, Justin, 29–31, 32, 35, 38

Wong, Jiverly, 62–63

Woodford, Jeanne, 26–27

writ of certiorari, 43

*Yale Law Journal,* 28

Zangara, Giuseppe, 50

# About the Author

Peggy J. Parks holds a bachelor of science degree from Aquinas College in Grand Rapids, Michigan, where she graduated magna cum laude. She has written more than 80 nonfiction educational books for children and young adults, as well as her own cookbook called *Welcome Home: Recipes, Memories, and Traditions from the Heart*. Parks lives in Muskegon, Michigan, a town that she says inspires her writing because of its location on the shores of Lake Michigan.